Pennsylvania's ALLEGHENY MOUNTAINS

Pennsylvania's ALLEGHENY MOUNTAINS

THE FIRST FRONTIER

DAVE HURST

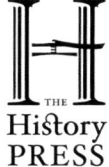

Published by The History Press
Charleston, SC 29403
www.historypress.net

Copyright © 2009 by Dave Hurst
All rights reserved

Cover images:
Front cover, top: *Country Road*, painted in 1878 by George Hetzel (1826–1899). *Westmoreland Museum of American Art, Greensburg, Pennsylvania, gift in memory of John H. Coulter by his friends and family.*
Front cover, bottom: Dr. Joseph Rothrock, Pennsylvania's "Father of Forestry," circa 1919. *Harris and Ewing Collection, Library of Congress.*

Back cover, left: Coal miners circa 1920. *Coal and Coke Heritage Center, Pennsylvania State University–Fayette, Eberly Campus, Hunchuck Collection.*
Back cover, right: The Battle of the Monongahela on July 5, 1755. *National Park Service, Fort Necessity National Battlefield.*

First published 2009
Second printing 2013

Manufactured in the United States

ISBN 978.1.59629.724.1

Library of Congress Cataloging-in-Publication Data

Hurst, Dave, 1952-
Pennsylvania's Allegheny Mountains : the first frontier / Dave Hurst.
p. cm.
ISBN 978-1-59629-724-1
1. Allegheny Mountains--History. 2. Allegheny Mountains--Anecdotes. 3. Pennsylvania--History. 4. Pennsylvania--Anecdotes. I. Title.
F157.A45H87 2009
974.8'7--dc22
2009025570

Notice: The information in this book is true and complete to the best of our knowledge. It is offered without guarantee on the part of the author or The History Press. The author and The History Press disclaim all liability in connection with the use of this book.

All rights reserved. No part of this book may be reproduced or transmitted in any form whatsoever without prior written permission from the publisher except in the case of brief quotations embodied in critical articles and reviews.

To God, who made this place and inspired this work.

*Wherever your footsteps
touch the earth,
a rich harvest is gathered.
Desert pastures blossom,
and mountains celebrate.*
—Psalms 65:11–12 CEV

Contents

Acknowledgements	11
Introduction	13

**Part I. The Nature of the Alleghenies:
    Pearl Fisheries and Hop Snow**

A State of Mind	19
At the Root of Penn's Woods	22
Seeing Through Visitors' Eyes	24
Proof that Our Heritage Is a Gem	26
Leaf-off Reconnaissance	28
Salty Talk on a Stormy Morning	31
Jumping Back to "Hop Snow"	34
Winter Is a Gift For the Soul	36
Many Names, One Place	37

**Part II. The People of the Alleghenies:
    A Peak and Valley Melting Pot**

What We Say Reflects Who We Are	43
Honoring the Scots-Irish	45
Happy Saint David's Day	47
Celebrate the Irish—For the Right Reasons	50
Underground Railroad Stories Are Surfacing	52
Faith Can Save Cambria City Churches	54

CONTENTS

Part III. When the Alleghenies Were Wilderness: World War, Whiskey Boys and George Washington

Hawkeye Was Here	57
Kittanning Trail Comes Alive	60
Our Elusive American Indian Story	63
History Can Teach Us about Us	65
Let's Remember November 25	67
Washington Wouldn't Approve of This	70
Johnny Appleseed Had Roots Here	72
Christmas by Candlelight	74

Part IV. Working with the Alleghenies: Transportation Unlocked the Treasure

It's No Bull: Plastic Grows on Cows	77
Our Window on the Past Is Open	80
Waterways Are Heritage Highways	82
Early Spring Is Canal-Trace Season	84
A Historic Landmark that Still Works	86
All the World Loved Connellsville Coke	88
Celebrate Coal Mining	90
The Year's First Sweet Reason to Travel	92
"Vanderbilt's Folly" Is Fun	94

Part V. Leisure in the Alleghenies: Gilded, Thrilling and Delicious

The Lure of Angling's Heritage	99
The Shape of Our Musical Heritage	101
Holidays of Early Advent	104
Mitchell Day	105
Lent Takes the Pagan to Church	108
A Great Old Story Gets New Wrinkles	109
The Alleghenies' Gilded Age	112
Classic Amusement	114
Try to Resist This Taste of Our Heritage	116
Appendix: Exploring Pennsylvania's Alleghenies	119
About the Author	127

Acknowledgements

While considering the opportunity offered by The History Press to publish a collection of my columns in book form, it was the publisher's request for dozens of illustrations that prompted my only hesitation. Much of my material is contemporary, yet the publisher wanted vintage illustrative material. Would I be able to find appropriate images in sufficient quantity and quality? Increasing the challenge was the understanding that all usage and processing fees would be paid for by the author. Many of the best images are preserved in historical archives, which cost nonprofit organizations money to house, staff and manage. Image processing and usage fees are entirely necessary and defensible—just unaffordable by me. Would I be able to find appropriate *gratis* images in sufficient quantity and quality?

Historical societies, museums and archives of south-central and southwestern Pennsylvania answered both questions with an overwhelmingly enthusiastic "Yes!" Contacts researched my often-vague requests and responded with illustrations or constructive suggestions of other places to look. They patiently scanned and sent multiple versions of their image files before achieving the publisher's specifications. Some were private individuals, who selflessly shared images from their personal collections. Other contacts were organizations that usually don't waive their image fees but did so in this instance.

These organizations and individuals contributed the illustrations that appear within these pages or assisted me in other ways: Allegheny Portage Railroad National Historic Site, Altoona Mirror, Berlin Area Historical

Acknowledgements

Society, Blairsville Area Historical Society, Blairsville Improvement Group, Blairsville Underground Railroad Museum, Bottle Works Ethnic Arts Center, Mike Burk, Cambria County Historical Society, Cambria Somerset Authority, Centre County Historical Society, Centre County Library and Historical Museum, Coal and Coke Heritage Center, Mitch Dakelman, Fort Necessity National Battlefield, Fort Ligonier, Fort Roberdeau, Gallitzin Borough, Donna Gambol, Huntingdon County Historical Society, Idlewild Park, Johnstown Area Heritage Association, Johnstown Flood National Memorial, Lakemont Park, Latrobe Area Historical Society, Library of Congress, Lincoln Highway Heritage Corridor, Russell Love, Larry McKee, Meyersdale Public Library, National Road Heritage Corridor, Old Bedford Village, Pennsylvania State Archives, Province of the Most Sacred Heart of Jesus (Franciscans Third Order Regular), Rivers of Steel National Heritage Area, Sacred Harp Publishing Company, Everett and Christine Sechler, David Seidel, Senator John Heinz History Center, Somerset Historical Center, Southern Alleghenies Conservancy, Southern Alleghenies Museum of Art, Springs Historical Society, Tyrone Area Historical Society, Village Restorations, Westmoreland Museum of American Art and Paula Zitzler.

The extraordinary contributions of the Westmoreland Museum of American Art deserve special recognition. Without WMAA's generosity and willingness to meet the more exacting requirements of cover images, the exterior of this book would be far less engaging.

The illustrations contributed by these organizations and individuals bring the stories of Pennsylvania's Allegheny Mountains to life. For that, and for their generosity, I am grateful. As you browse this book, pay attention to the credit lines and—if you have the opportunity—tell the contributing organization or individual that you saw their image. I can think of no better way to repay their graciousness.

Introduction

Pennsylvania's Allegheny Mountains have always had an identity problem. In our earliest histories, they were reviled as hulking wilderness landmasses that stood in the way of westward travel and hid savage natives in the dark shade of their old-growth forests. When shown on many of the oldest maps, they were labeled "Allegheny" by the French and "Allegany" by the English. During the Industrial Revolution, they were valued only for their natural resources. Virgin timber was stripped from ridges and valleys alike. Coal and minerals were ripped from the landscape and replaced with waste piles of boney and slag. Streams were choked with acidic, metals-laden mine discharge, agricultural runoff and raw sewage. Immigrants settled here—in part—because the Alleghenies reminded them of similar hills and mountains in Wales, Ireland, Ruthenia and other Old World homelands. Today, with the subsidence of manufacturing and mining (and the maturing of second-growth forests), this landscape is recovering much of its original beauty and vitality. Increasingly, these ridges are becoming recognized for their natural and cultural heritage–based recreational opportunities. Yet no one seems quite certain exactly where the Allegheny Mountains are in Pennsylvania.

As far as geologists are concerned, the Allegheny Mountains don't exist. The Appalachians are the only real mountain range in the eastern United States. Within the central Appalachian Mountains in Pennsylvania are two geological provinces: the Valley and Ridge Province and the Appalachian Plateau. Dividing them is the Allegheny Front—the only "Allegheny" formation recognized by geology. The Allegheny Mountains are not actually

Introduction

mountains, either. They are ribs of harder bedrock that resisted erosion within the Appalachian Plateau. The Alleghenies weren't raised—surrounding land was lowered.

Geographically, however, the Allegheny Mountains clearly have their place. Maps show them extending from northern Pennsylvania to southwestern Virginia. Their east–west boundaries are not as easily defined—especially in Pennsylvania. Geographers suggest that the "Alleghenies" should include only the landforms to the west of the Allegheny Front—the Allegheny, Laurel and Chestnut Ridges along with a broad plateau extending from north-central through southwestern Pennsylvania. Yet governmental groups and tourism-promotion agencies have been applying the "Alleghenies" name to landforms east of the Front—such as Tussey and Jacks Mountains—even though those landforms belong to a different geological province. Adding further to the confusion, the area with the strongest claim to the Alleghenies label calls itself the Laurel Highlands instead.

Then there's the general disagreement about how to spell the name. The states of New York and Maryland use the "Allegany" spelling for names of counties, forests and parks, whereas Pennsylvania prefers the French spelling and applies it to all references (including the mountains, river and national forest) in Pennsylvania. "Allegheny" is the accepted spelling for the river, even in New York State, and for the mountain range to the south of Pennsylvania.

Pennsylvania's Allegheny Mountains are scenically beautiful, especially when robed in summer's verdancy or autumn's variegation. But this book isn't just about this region's natural heritage. Pennsylvania's Alleghenies were ancient when the Leni-Lenape crossed their rugged flanks along deer paths, when a young George Washington touched off a world war here and when the first Europeans settled in sheltered hollows. But this book isn't just about the national—even international—significance of history here. These ridges determined transportation corridors and yielded rich mineral resources that supplied much of America's Industrial Revolution. They shaped fortunes, drew immigrants and nurtured faiths. But this book isn't just about the region's cultural heritage. A getaway since Americans have been taking vacations, these Alleghenies are once again drawing people who are looking for stimulating ways to spend their leisure time. But this book isn't just a recreational guide.

This is a collection of newspaper columns written over six years that, at one time or another, touch on all of these topics within a regional context

Introduction

that embraces the broadest-possible cultural delineation of the Alleghenies: essentially the southwestern quarter of Pennsylvania from Centre, Huntingdon and Fulton Counties west to the state boundary with West Virginia. As such, this work seeks to capture the essence of this place, which is more than the sum of its geological, geographical, historical, cultural and recreational parts. There is a spirit here—a quality of life—that is rooted in the rugged landscape, the friendliness and traditional values found here and the bond between this place and its people. It's a quality that may not be immediately apparent to some. It certainly wasn't to me.

Although the year was 1979, I still remember my first impression of the region vividly. It wasn't a good one. I had traveled to Johnstown to interview for a radio-news position and had observed that the highway into town was tracked with coal dust from tri-axled trucks, thundering in both directions, and that the old steel mill across the river gave the city a dirty, dingy look. The early November timing of my interview didn't help. Stripped of its leafage, the landscape was dreary, weary from another growing season and ready for winter slumber.

Not that I cared much. At that time, my name for this place was "stepping stone." I was young and ambitious, a broadcast journalist aiming for the big markets—maybe the networks. I wouldn't be here long anyway, I thought. During the initial years, my career plan seemed to be working. I shifted from radio to a CBS television affiliate in Altoona. I worked hard, honed my craft—even tried to get my straight, thin hair under control with perms—then started sending out resumes and audition tapes.

Meanwhile, my family was growing. A firstborn son was joined by a sister and then a brother. I found myself appreciating how they could play in a neighborhood where everyone watched out for one another. As they reached school age, my kids entered a small but dispersed school district where they received personal attention and made friends from other neighborhoods all over town—safe, solid neighborhoods, populated with caring people who treated my kids as their own.

As dozens of resumes were going out, I was running these ridges and covering news stories of all types, meeting people and seeing the beauty that changing seasons imposed on the rugged terrain: the subtle vibrancy of spring's pastels; the lush green scenes of summer; autumn's acrylic artistry; and even winter's soft snowfalls and crystalline ice shows. As "heritage development" stories emerged in the late 1980s and early 1990s, I started to learn about the nationally significant events that had occurred here: the French and Indian

Introduction

War, the Whiskey Rebellion and the National Road; the Pennsylvania Main Line Canal and Pennsylvania Railroad; coal, Connellsville coke and the birth of integrated steelmaking; the Johnstown Flood; and more. I met colorful union coal miners, third-generation steelworkers and the children of emigrants from Europe, the Mediterranean and Africa, admired their achievements and observed how much they accomplished through faith in God and hard work. My stories documented the efforts of innovative planners and industrious volunteers who were working to preserve historical buildings and districts, clean up industrial pollution and develop heritage sites, special events, rail-trails and other recreational resources. Over and over, my experiences revealed that this region was and is a striking place, a storied place, a family-friendly place, an invigorating place and a place that visitors would enjoy.

I found myself wondering why I wanted to leave. Resumes stopped going out. My concentration shifted to merging my professional path with my growing passion for the natural and cultural heritage of Pennsylvania's Alleghenies. The Altoona television reporter became a Johnstown newspaper reporter and then editor of a regional magazine titled *Westsylvania* (a name that frontiersmen wanted to call this place back in the late eighteenth century), based in Hollidaysburg. My interest in—and my writing about—the region went from casual to part time to full time. Then in 2003, after stepping out on my own path as a full-time freelancer, I launched a syndicated newspaper column that explores our Allegheny Mountains' heritage on a weekly basis. It is a selection of those columns that are published within these pages.

This book is not offered as a comprehensive history of the Alleghenies but rather as a collection of thoughts on what makes this region and its people unique. Some of these vignettes are cerebral. Others present interesting places, events or activities within their historical contexts. While these columns are written to be an entertaining read, their goal is to inspire you to learn more about this fascinating, richly textured, multifaceted place and to experience it for yourself. A staple of the newspaper versions of the columns is to offer suggestions on sites to visit, events to enjoy and other activities that will enable you to sample the subject yourself. But that approach presents a challenge in book format, where commonly used information, such as specific dates, phone numbers and website URLs (all of which frequently change), should be avoided so as to keep the book from quickly becoming dated. So while the vignettes published here are based on columns that originally may have been published as early as 2003, each has been updated and edited to

Introduction

emphasize the historical context of the subject. In the appendix you will find useable listings of events, sites, agencies and addresses that you can plug into your favorite Internet search engine to obtain the current information needed to experience these topics for yourself.

So join me in Pennsylvania's Allegheny Mountains. You'll be fascinated by the stories preserved here, the refreshing ways you can experience them and the fun you can have doing it.

PART I

The Nature of the Alleghenies

Pearl Fisheries and Hop Snow

There may be confusion over which landforms actually are the Alleghenies, but this is a distinct place with a unique natural heritage. Perhaps its ridges don't meet the geological definition of being mountains, but they certainly are mountainous in character. Whoever coined the phrase "ridge runner" never tried to scramble up these rocky, steep-sloped formations. Yet one reward for doing so is to absorb the seeming agelessness of this place.

While the Industrial Revolution stripped the Alleghenies of their old-growth hardwoods, we still have a sense of what American Indian eyes saw here through the expansive secondary growth that has replaced it. Overlooks reveal scenic summer panoramas of rippling, lush greenery that erupt into flaming foliage in autumn. Seasons here are vivid, offering occasional tableaux that are spectacular. As you become more familiar with their past and get to know their character, though, and you'll learn that the Alleghenies offer more than just a pretty face.

A State of Mind

A reader e-mailed me a few years ago, objecting to my use of the name "Westsylvania" in my newspaper column. "Just remember there is no such place," the reader wrote. "If you would like to change the name of the area we live in, then you move and create that place somewhere else…"

Pennsylvania's Allegheny Mountains

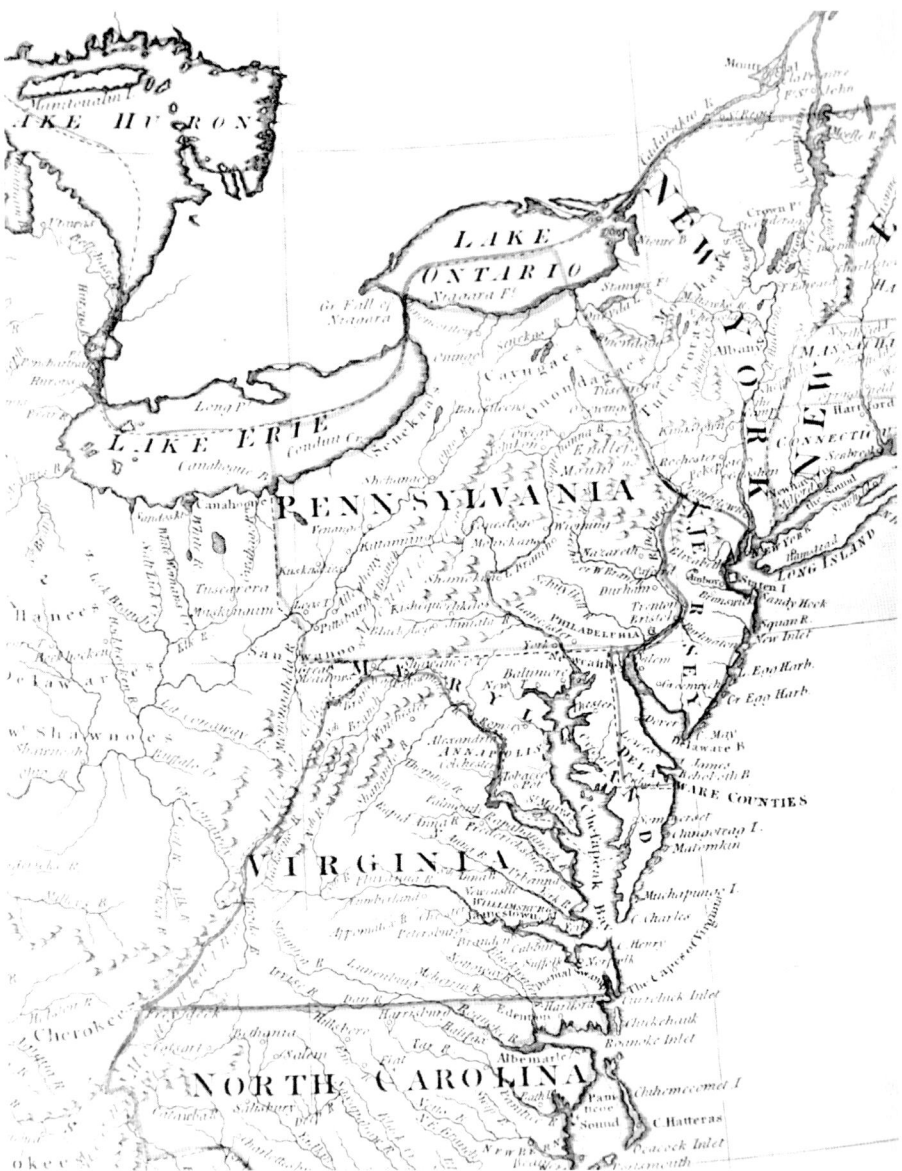

A map of the United States circa 1783, showing the indistinct boundary between Pennsylvania and Virginia. *Pennsylvania State Archives, MG-11, Map 463.*

The First Frontier

While always glad for reader feedback—affirmative or negative—I was especially appreciative of this one, because it reminded me that many do not know the origins of the name "Westsylvania." The year was 1776, and this was the western frontier—much of it just opened to settlement eight years earlier by the "New Purchase" arranged with the Iroquois at Fort Stanwix. Only two counties—Bedford and Westmoreland—existed within the region then. The border between them was Laurel Hill. An estimated twenty-five thousand families were already living here, scratching a rough existence from the hardwoods that covered the land, huddling around stone hearths during cold winters and fearing deadly raids by displaced natives. Those west of Laurel Hill weren't sure if they were in Pennsylvania or Virginia—both colonies had been selling tracts of land in what Governor William Penn called Westmoreland County and what Virginia Governor, Lord Dunmore, considered the District of West Augusta. Conflicting jurisdictional claims and transactions caused much turmoil, but neither provincial government did much to protect or supply the settlers.

"[I]rritated & exasperated by ills & urged & compelled by oppressions & sufferings, and having imbibed the highest & most extensive Ideas of Liberty," almost two thousand frontiersmen signed a petition in July 1776 asking the Continental Congress to establish an independent fourteenth colony "under the Name of—'the Province & Government of Westsylvania.'"

Concerned that consideration would escalate boundary tensions between Pennsylvania and Virginia at a time when the colonies needed to remain united against Great Britain, the Continental Congress buried the petition in a committee. But residents' desires to create a new state persisted for the rest of the eighteenth century and was one of the root causes of the Whiskey Rebellion in 1794—an uprising as much about self-governance as about a tax on the region's chief export.

"Westsylvania," although preserved faintly in scattered histories, largely disappeared from public awareness until 1997, when it became the name of a small regional magazine and, later, of the Hollidaysburg-based organization that published it. (At that time, I was editor of the magazine.) But the spirit of Westsylvania—hardiness, courage, independence and innovative self-sufficiency in the face of immense natural and cultural challenges—has never left our region. Its symbols include the Allegheny Portage Railroad, the Horseshoe Curve, Mount Etna Iron Furnace, Cambria Ironworks, the Edgar Thomson steel mill, the beehive coke ovens of the Connellsville region and the Three Rivers' locks and dams. You can find it along the Kittanning

Trail, Forbes Road, the National Road and Lincoln Highway. The spirit of Westsylvania was embodied by German Brethren who farmed the fertile but feral land, by Irish laborers who carved railways over and through the Alleghenies, by African American steelworkers who worked the closest to the blast furnace's inferno, by Italian miners who laid in thirty-six-inch seams shoveling coal and by Slovak mothers raising six kids in four rooms.

Nor is the Westsylvania spirit only present in our past. Today it fills small entrepreneurs creating their own jobs; conservationists building wetlands to eliminate abandoned-mine drainage from our streams; volunteers developing and maintaining recreation trails; and heritage-site operators and heritage-event promoters who persevere in presenting what makes our region unique.

The facts describe Westsylvania as a concept for a new state that never materialized. But as a state of mind that has shaped this region for centuries, Westsylvania exists.

First published in February 2004.

At the Root of Penn's Woods

Is it possible to miss the old-growth forest for the trees? I pondered that question while walking briskly but tentatively along a beautiful little brook called Detweiler Run in the Rothrock State Forest—briskly because I was losing daylight, tentatively because despite the rocky trail my eyes kept looking up to see what Dr. Joseph Trimbel Rothrock might have seen one hundred years ago: old-growth trees that count their ages and heights in the hundreds. Rothrock is considered the "Father of Forestry" in Pennsylvania. He was appointed to head a new Division of Forestry in 1895 and launched a land-acquisition program that led to the establishment of the state forest system.

Many of us take Pennsylvania's state forests for granted. There are nineteen statewide. Each is managed by a district forester and staff responsible for control of fire and insects and the management of timber, habitat, water and recreation. Parts of five state forests exist within our region: Tuscarora and Rothrock (Huntingdon County), Buchanan (Fulton and Bedford Counties), Gallitzin (Bedford, Somerset and Cambria Counties) and Forbes (Somerset, Westmoreland and Fayette Counties).

The First Frontier

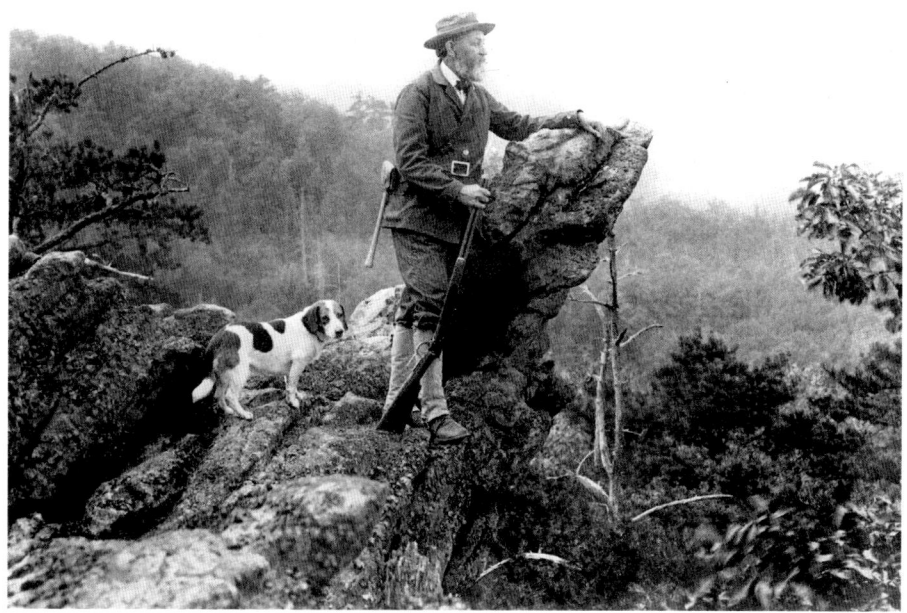

Dr. Joseph Rothrock was a medical doctor, botanist and Pennsylvania's "Father of Forestry." Shown here with a companion circa 1919. *Harris and Ewing Collection, Library of Congress.*

Our state park system gets most of the public's recreational attention, yet the state forest system offers more varied recreational opportunities. You can hunt, fish, hike, picnic and ride horses, mountain bikes, ATVs and snowmobiles on state forest land. And state forests cover some of the state's most spectacular landscape. Within its boundaries are sixty-one designated natural areas and sixteen designated wild areas, where special plants and animals are protected and nature has its way.

I was working my way upstream within the Detweiler Run Natural Area in a hollow of a region known as Seven Mountains. Look at the center of Pennsylvania on a relief map. Imagine that as God was forming this particular part of the earth he stuck in a slotted spoon here and gave a stir. The result was Seven Mountains. Man stripped the trees from its many slopes to feed the ravenous Greenwood iron-making furnaces in the late 1800s. When that industry cooled, Rothrock acquired most of the Seven Mountains for the state. So verdant with maples, oak, poplar, hemlock and white pine are these mountains today, it's hard to even see surrounding ridge tops much less imagine them clear-cut. The growth in this hollow was so lush and thick that trees more than one hundred feet tall could hide here. Still searching for old growth, I pushed on.

Perseverance paid off as a massive white pine came into view along the right side of the trail. Easily eight feet in circumference, the tree's thick trunk tapered little even as it divided about sixty feet above. The crown wasn't visible, and I could only wonder at the tree's height. A short distance farther stood a majestic hemlock, its trunk too thick for two people to reach around, its boughs radiating symmetrically upward. Finally, I reached an old-growth oratory—gothic in the day's dying light—with straight, tall columns of white pine and arched with hemlock boughs. Only rhododendron worshipped within.

Rothrock may well have stood in such a place, contemplating the loss of such trees, knowing that a century or more would be needed to replace them and wondering perhaps if man would ever exercise such patience. Whether such a sight inspired Rothrock to begin to grow Penn's Woods anew—and to better manage them—this place certainly affirms his efforts.

Thanks to the state forest system, such affirming places are near you. Seek them out. Discover what once was—and may, someday, become again.

First published in August 2003.

Seeing Through Visitors' Eyes

"This is so beautiful," said Tom, his tone suggesting that he was deep in memories. My longtime friend and I were spending a rare day together on an improvisational road trip around southwestern Pennsylvania. Although a southwestern Pennsylvania native, Tom lives in the Phoenix, Arizona suburb of Scottsdale, and his trips back east are annual at best. Accustomed to the desert perspectives of the Southwest, he was getting an almost vernal look at our well-watered greenery. "This is so beautiful," Tom kept repeating, as we drove east along the National Road (U.S. Route 40) through Scenery Hill, as we crested Laurel Hill on PA Route 31 and returned by way of the Loyalhanna Gorge along the Lincoln Highway (U.S. Route 30).

Haven't you heard a visitor rave about our region's natural beauty? Seeing our countryside constantly, as we do, it's understandable that our senses become dulled to the splendor of our rugged, hardwooded ridges and valleys—until we see it afresh through other eyes. But our constant exposure

The First Frontier

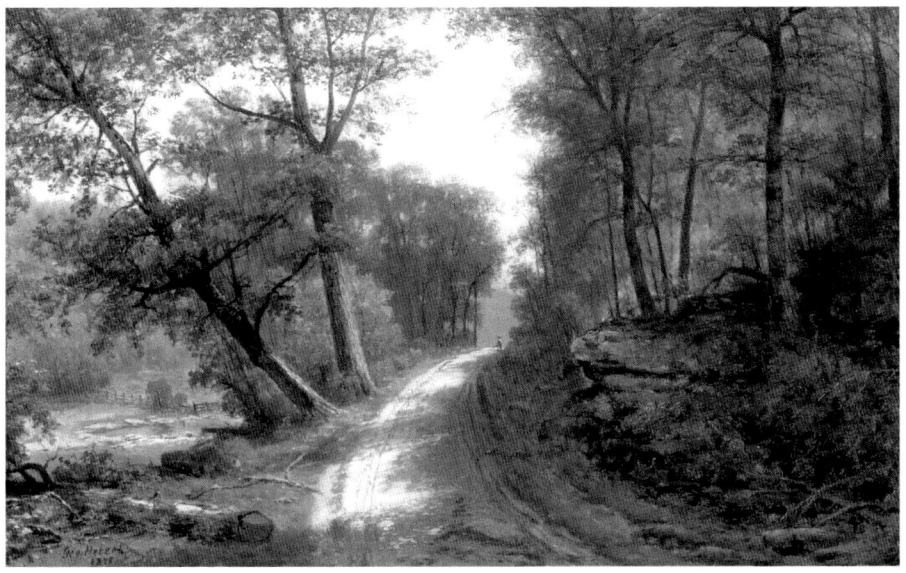

Country Road by George Hetzel, 1878, oil on canvas. *Westmoreland Museum of American Art, Greensburg, Pennsylvania. Gift in memory of John H. Coulter by his friends and family.*

also puts us in the position to witness those ethereal moments when landscape and light and weather conditions meet in magical convention.

On another day the view from the commercial hilltop in Johnstown's suburban East Hills commanded me to pull the car over and pay attention. I was looking westward on this early September morning as a front of dapple-gray clouds marched to the northeast at a steady cadence. Laurel Ridge remained somewhat shrouded by the morning mist. Hollows, where the Conemaugh Valley rose to meet the Allegheny Plateau, had not yet released their captive wisps to the rising sun. Flanking the cloud columns were scattered patches of soft blue sky, allowing rays of sunlight to splay along the undulating landscape. A farm field was spotlighted in one place, a cluster of country homes set against a wooded hillside in another. There was a Wagnerian grandeur to the scene's deep, uncertain mood. Then, the clouds closed ranks. The sunlight and the moment were gone.

Such moments are not uncommon here, but they are difficult to capture and should be savored when encountered. Spend some time trying to photograph our scenic beauty and you'll discover its elusiveness. Weather conditions often are uncooperative, haze may mute the panorama, the sun may be in the wrong place and so on. Usually, only those who are gifted, possessing good equipment and committed to spending the necessary time, capture the scenes successfully.

Experiences such as these have taught me to treasure the beautiful vistas and special moments created when season and light and landscape conspire. Encountering them now, I stop whatever I'm doing and enjoy them, even if just for a minute or two. The amount of time spent is less important than the decision to make the time—to experience sunlight filtering through the yellow leaves in a stand of poplar, the crimson spray of sumac along the roadside or the mosaic of reds and oranges, greens and burgundies across a hardwooded hillside. Five minutes spent in consideration of the mists, rising to meet the brooding cumulus on a rapidly warming morning, can be as spiritually uplifting as a day hike along a valley brook, where the scent of rich loam dances on the breeze with a falling leaf.

As we enter what often proves to be our most spectacular season, promise yourself to take a moment, an hour, a day to appreciate the Alleghenies' natural beauty. Look with fresh eyes on our common place—a place that visitors find remarkable—and be on the lookout for those mystical moments that are among God's blessings for living here.

First published in October 2003.

Proof that Our Heritage Is a Gem

One of the things that makes our region's history so interesting is what one finds after fishing around a bit. Doing some research for a client recently, I came upon this excerpt from a 1905 Cambria County newspaper article, quoted in the "Bicentennial Commemorative History of Loretto, Pennsylvania":

> *A pearl found some time ago in an old lake on the campus of St. Francis College, Loretto, is described by a New York City jewelry concern as the finest Pennsylvania gem of that kind ever sent to them for mounting.*

Whoa. "A pearl...the finest Pennsylvania gem of that kind..." We have pearls in Pennsylvania? Gemology admittedly is far from my forte, but don't pearls come from the seas of the Far East? Some quick research answered that question. Turns out that pearls can be produced by mollusks in both

The First Frontier

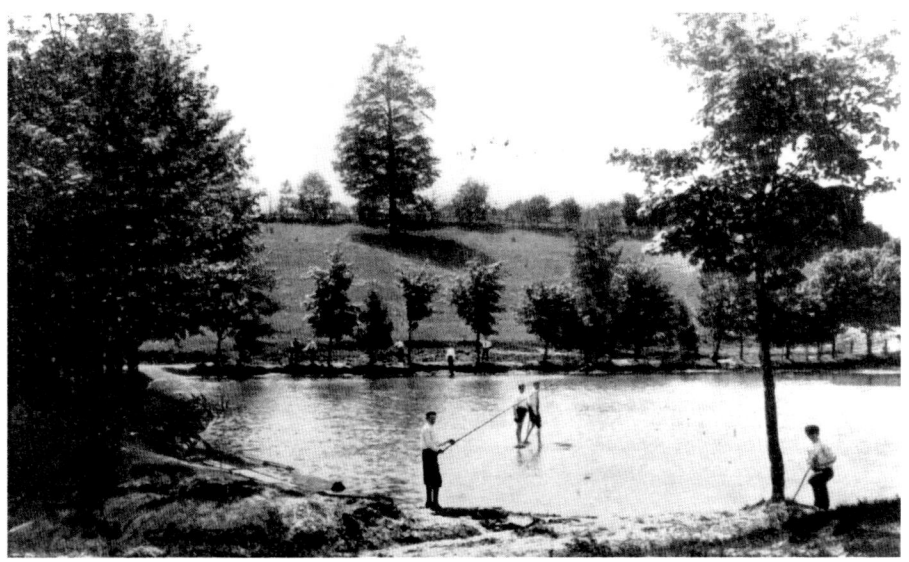

Students fish and wade at Lake Saint Francis in a scene dating to the early 1900s. *Photograph reproduced with permission from the Third Order Regular Franciscan Archives.*

salt water and fresh water. And before the development of the cultured-pearl industry in the Far East during the 1920s, America had a worldwide reputation for producing fine freshwater pearls (and mother-of-pearl materials such as buttons made from the lining of mussel shells).

Both natural and cultured pearls are produced in the same way, whether in fresh water or salt water: the mollusk encases an irritant with nacre, thus producing the pearl. However, the natural pearl is produced by accident and is almost 100 percent nacre, whereas the cultured pearl begins with an implanted bead and contains much less nacre. But were natural freshwater pearls produced in Pennsylvania—and, more specifically, in our region? The Internet had nothing to say about that question, so I tried the Pennsylvania Fish and Boat Commission and discovered that there is a staff malacologist, a biologist who specializes in mollusks.

Malacologist Nevin Welte had never heard of pearl fisheries in western Pennsylvania, but he believes it could have been possible. Most species of mussels, he explained, are capable of producing pearls, and surveys conducted by the Carnegie Museum in the early 1900s documented an abundance and great variety of mussels throughout Pennsylvania's lakes and river systems. Unfortunately, Pennsylvania's rapid industrialization during that same period polluted many of its waterways and wreaked havoc on the sensitive mollusk populations. Today, most species of mussels are considered endangered in Pennsylvania, and commercial harvesting for mother-of-pearl production is not permitted here. Welte knows of only one section of the Schuylkill River system in eastern Pennsylvania where a "reproductively viable population" of freshwater pearl mussel still exists.

Yet, if the 1905 newspaper article is to be believed, pearls had been found in the small lake on the campus at Saint Francis—including an unusually fine one, salmon-colored and perfectly shaped, discovered by a Franciscan friar named Brother Joseph Conway. Then, as today, Saint Francis was a Franciscan school. Having taken a vow of poverty, Brother Joseph couldn't cash in on the gem. Instead, he gave it to a neighbor and friend, Emma Schwab. Emma was the wife of Charles Schwab, a steel industry titan who had been raised in Loretto and educated at Saint Francis and who maintained a summer home across the road from the campus. Mrs. Schwab sent the pearl to Tiffany & Co. of New York to have it mounted into a platinum ring, and it was Tiffany's that documented its quality, according to the article. "Mrs. Schwab thinks more of Brother Joseph's pearl than all the diamonds I ever gave her," Charles Schwab reportedly told a friend, according to the article.

"It's very rare for any freshwater mussels to have a pearl of significant quality," Nevin told me, "especially if Tiffany's found it noteworthy; that's wild."

To me the story is a fascinating glimpse of how different our homeland was less than one hundred years ago—and another revealing facet of the gem that is our region's heritage.

First published in October 2007.

Leaf-off Reconnaissance

"Don't tell anyone, but I think this is the most beautiful spot in the park." Nancy Smith of the National Park Service offers that opinion as we stand on an access road in the heart of the Allegheny Portage Railroad National Historic Site.

Sorry, Nancy. I'm paid to have a big mouth. We're looking across a picturesque, hardwooded hollow of the Allegheny Front above Altoona but well below the Cresson Summit. Traffic along old U.S. Route 22 is more audible than visible several hundred yards in front of us. Between us and

The First Frontier

U.S. 22, vigorous streamlets of Blair Gap Run wrap through the woods and join joyously. Sunlight soaks a landscape covered only by still-barren trees. Midmorning's temperature is in the soul-satisfying upper sixties. This moment alone would be worth the mile-and-a-half walk along the access from Valley Forge Road. But we're here to see Culvert 1532 on Level Nine.

Between 1834 and 1854, the Allegheny Portage Railroad was a critical component of the Pennsylvania Main Line System of Public Works, a system of railroads and canals that transported people and freight between Philadelphia and Pittsburgh. This was the state-of-the-art rapid-transit system of the day, covering in four days the distance that required twenty-three days for wagons. The Allegheny Portage Railroad lifted Pennsylvania Canal passengers and freight over the Allegheny Front with a system of ten inclines and eleven levels. Numbering started in Johnstown with Level One and Incline One and ended with Incline 10 and Level 11 extending into Hollidaysburg.

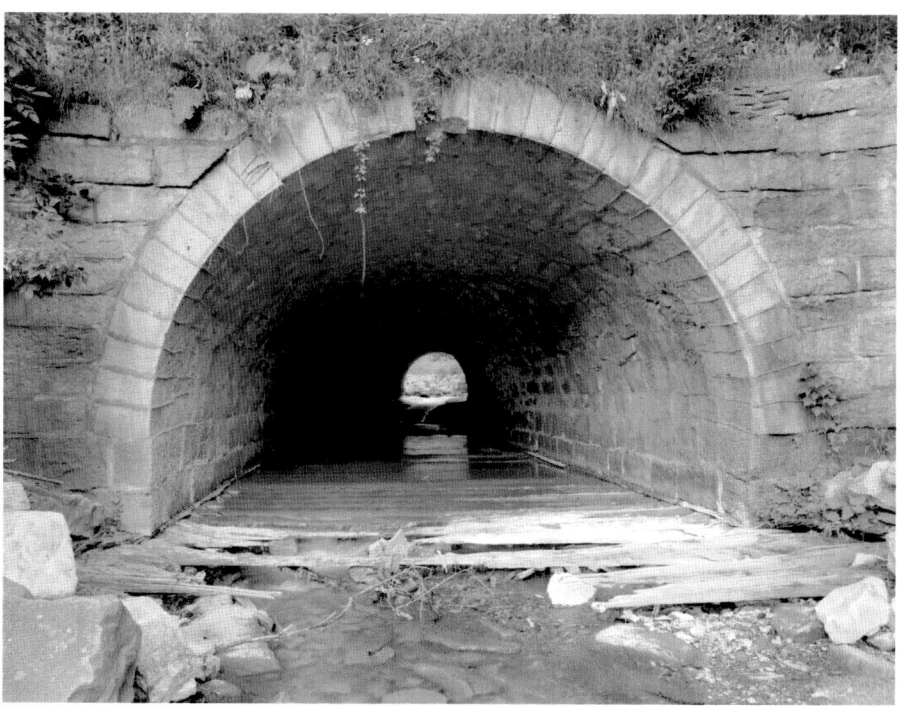

An Allegheny Portage Railroad culvert built in 1832 spans Bens Creek at PA 53 in Cassandra. *Photograph by Joseph Elliott, Historic American Engineering Record, Library of Congress.*

With the landscape still leafless, we can easily follow the line of Level Nine as it approaches us along the floor of the hollow, crosses Culvert 1532 and bumps against the base of the bench where Nancy and I had just enjoyed the sylvan view. Culvert 1532—the number goes back to the Allegheny Portage days—really looks more like a short, single-arch stone bridge. Although rebuilt by the park service in 2000, the culvert's original "barrel"—the underbelly of the arch made of dry-laid (without mortar) cut-stone—remains intact after 170 years. There is temptation to linger here, to dwell on that craftsmanship and the almost unimaginable labor implied.

Instead, let's consider the special character of this time of year in our region. At Allegheny Portage, park service people call this period "leaf-off." Its brevity makes it precious. When the last of the Allegheny ridge snow pack disappears, there may be only three weeks or so before lush green foliage bursts forth and clothes the landscape. Yes, our greenery is beautiful. It rivals any, anywhere. But it also covers the rugged qualities and interesting stories of our Alleghenies. During leaf-off, though, we can easily see how men, working only with black powder, muscle and horses, leveled valleys and split ridge ribs for the Portage Railroad. We can see the small, cut-stone retaining walls, foundations and ground depressions that hint of engine houses, hitching sheds and other structures.

The same is true where you live, too. This is the time when you can read the stories of your local landscape. Meander along a river bank and look for canal traces. Wander the site of a frontier fort, an abandoned coal patch or a tumbled-down gristmill. Use your imagination, pictures or memories to visualize what once stood there. Stand beside a merrily trickling rill, close your eyes and feel the sun-warmed breeze. Study a limestone block shaped by hand and, at its base, a bright-yellow coltsfoot shaped by the Master Craftsman.

Respect private property, of course, and revere the resource. Leave no trace of your time spent there and leave with nothing that you didn't bring with you. Leaf-off reconnaissance offers something far more valuable than some interesting artifact that quickly becomes clutter. Its prizes are lessons about time and place—and an injection of spring for your soul.

First published in April 2003.

The First Frontier

Salty Talk on a Stormy Morning

It's the morning after a night of wind and rain, and leaving the house for work, you notice a small patch of blue sky through a break in the sooty, roiled clouds. Almost instinctively you feel a sense of hope that the weather's going to get better. There's an old weather bromide that roots this hope.

"The skies will clear if there's enough blue sky to make a Dutchman's breeches," my friend and fellow church-member, Fran Jacobs, told me.

"That's right," chimed in Mary Cay Ruddock, a frequent Fran collaborator. "'A Dutchman's breeches,' I heard that, too, as a little girl."

These ladies know I'm interested in local weather folklore and had recalled this particular saying. My response was a stupid-sounding "Dutchman's breeches?"

"You know, pants," responded Fran in the same animated voice she uses with the church's kids.

Pants…Dutchman's breeches…blue sky? Okay, we've a lot of Pennsylvania Germans around here—German Catholics, Amish, Mennonites and Wesleyan German-Protestants, such as the Evangelicals who founded my church. This could be some type of regional saying.

My research took me to the website of the Mount Washington Observatory of North Conway, New Hampshire. Mount Washington is the highest peak in the northeastern United States and self-proclaimed "home of the world's worst weather…where people are on hand to take measurements." Because its 6,288-foot summit lies in the path of principal storm tracks and air-mass routes, Mount Washington's annual-average temperature (26.5 degrees), snowfall (256 inches) and fog-days (over three hundred) make Cresson, Clyde and Ogletown seem almost semitropical by comparison. So it should come as no surprise that Mount Washington's staff is really into the subject of weather and enjoys researching weather questions.

Staff member Rebecca Peterman responded to my inquiry about blue sky and Dutchman's breeches. According to Rebecca's research, the saying originated as a British sailors' slur on the Dutch, probably fueled by the Anglo-Dutch naval wars of the seventeenth and eighteenth centuries. The British caricatured the Dutch as wearing big baggy pants—ergo, if there seemed to be enough blue in the sky to make a pair of baggy breeches, sailors observed that the weather would clear.

Until researching this expression, I hadn't considered how many Dutch-related expressions that we commonly use carry negative connotations. We

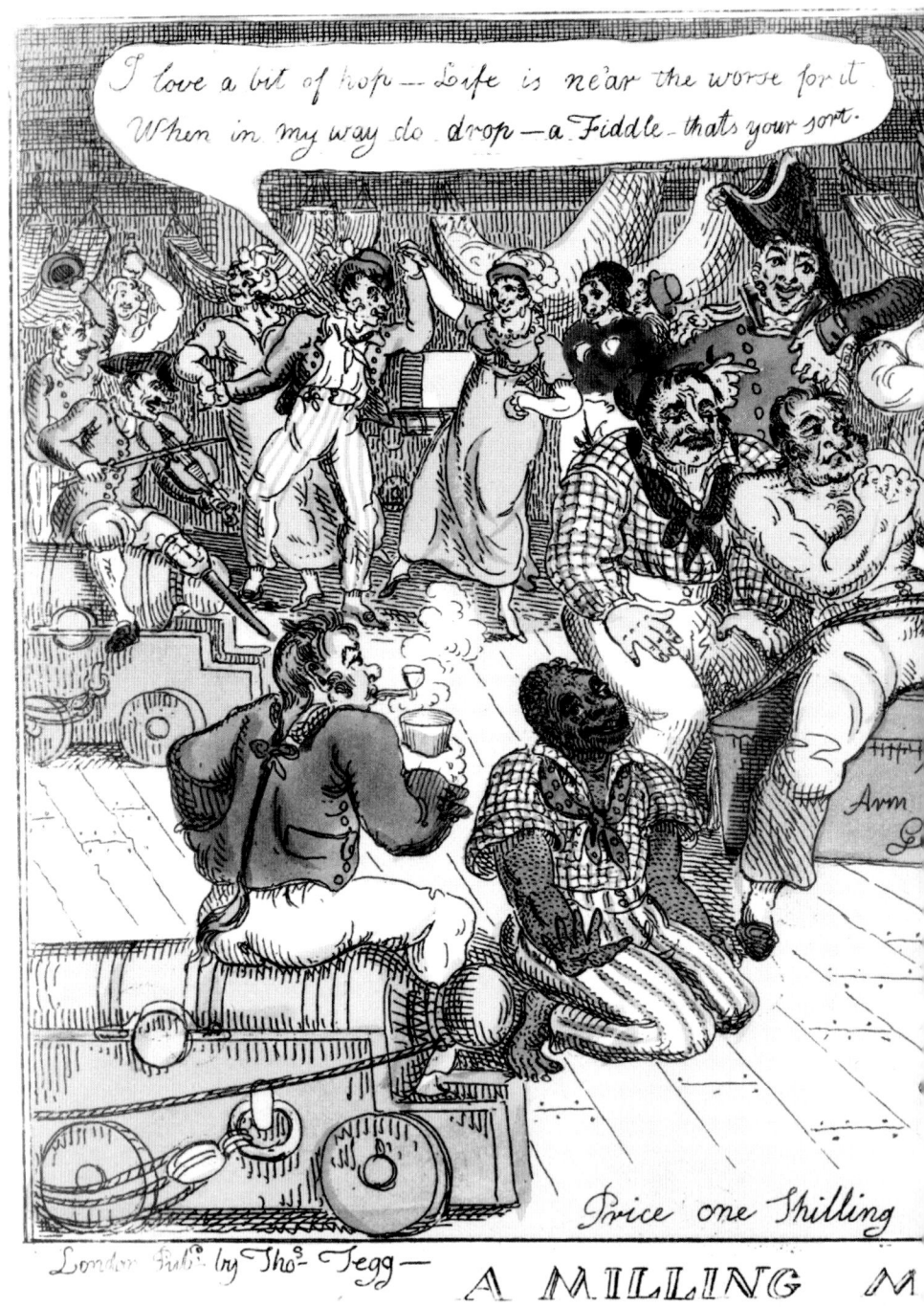

An etching of a cartoon depicting British sailors circa 1810–20. *British Cartoon Prints Collection of the Library of Congress.*

The First Frontier

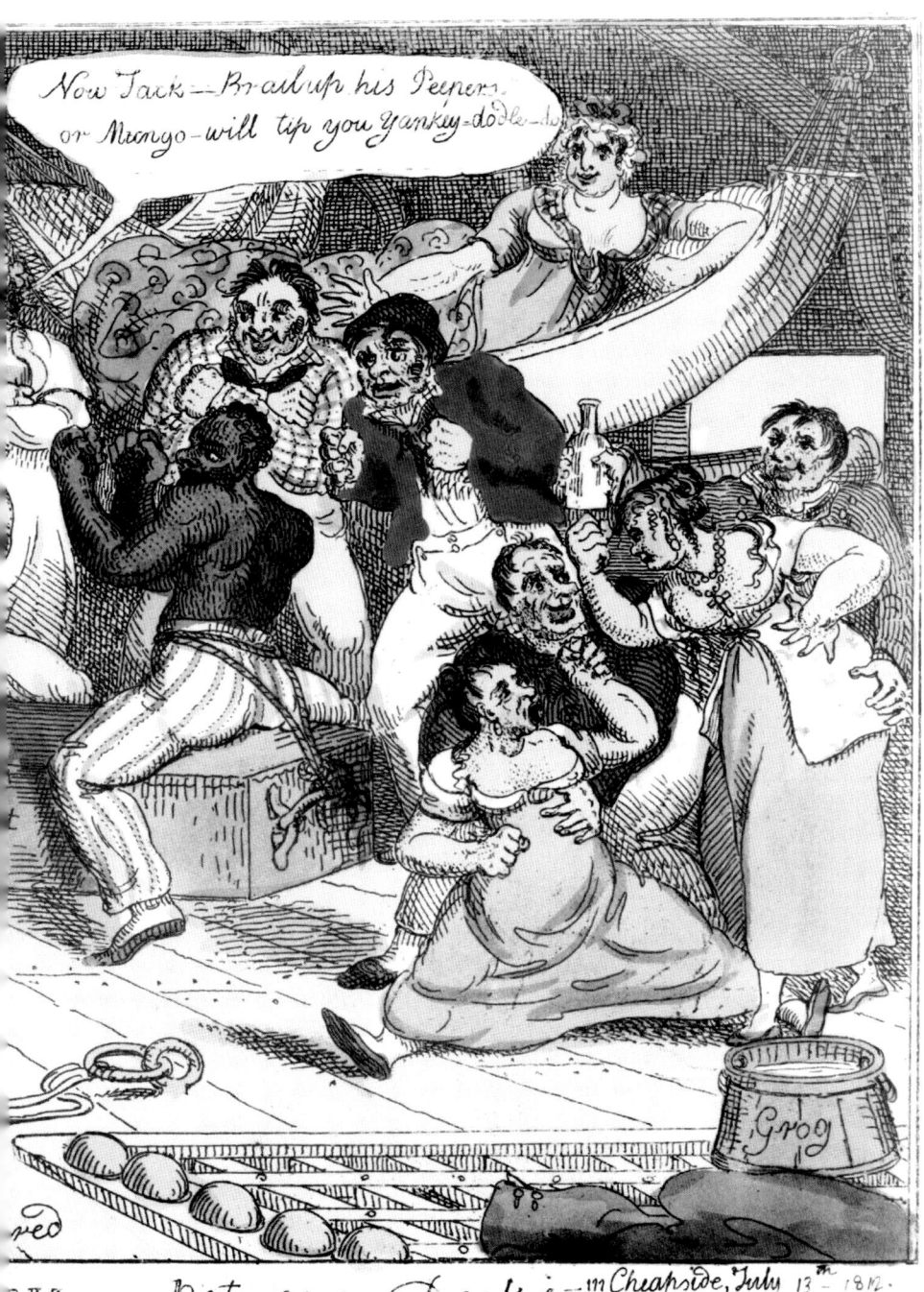

refer to Dutch uncles (stern advisors), getting "in Dutch" (trouble) and Dutch generosity and Dutch treat (stinginess). What have the Dutch ever done to us? Nothing of which I'm aware—in fact their assistance to us during the American Revolution was the cause of the fourth and final Anglo-Dutch War. Yet this blue-sky saying and other Dutch-inflected expressions reflect the passions of an all-but-forgotten, three-hundred-year-old conflict.

What a treasure house of heritage is our language! Often our expressions—especially those that we consider cliché—have interesting storylines extending back over hundreds of years. That they are cliché today underscores how widely they've spread and how extensively they've been used over that time. How did this British nautical disparagement of the Dutch come to our region? Likely the same way that it spread elsewhere in our country: as a weather observation made by neighbor to neighbor, mother to daughter, traveler to traveler. I can't wait to tell my church ladies about their salty language.

First published in November 2005. My thanks to the hardy folks at Mount Washington Observatory for their help.

Jumping Back to "Hop Snow"

Regional stories of epic scale have been explored in this column from time to time. Tales of international intrigue during the French and Indian War, of the heroic endurance of immigrant miners and millworkers, of visionary efforts to preserve our cultural heritage and of the innovative coalitions restoring our natural heritage—just to name a few. But the topic that has prompted far more reader feedback than any other is…drumroll, please… "hop snow."

This all started after I heard a couple of friends use the term "hop snow" and invited readers to tell me what they knew of the phrase. Dozens of readers replied with e-mail and traditional mail, all agreeing that it was the name of a snowfall in the spring. On the origin of "hop snow," though, there was a lot of head-scratching, and on its meaning there were diverse opinions. That it referred to snowflakes literally hopping as they landed on the spring-warmed ground was a popular belief. I published this speculation in a follow-up column, which prompted several more notes from readers—and, perhaps, a more authoritative answer.

The First Frontier

"I gave my 90-year-old father your column and asked him about it," wrote Ellen Vorhauer of Johnstown. "He said the 'hops snow' was considered the last snow of the spring, usually in mid- to late-April, about the time when the hops plants were starting to come out of the ground." Hops plants? As in "barley, malt and hops" in beer? Yep. But generations ago, hops were used for more than just brewing. "Hops were grown by many families prior to refrigeration and used to make the yeast for baking bread," explained Vorhauer.

Mark Ware of the Somerset Historical Center—where hops grow in an herb garden—describes the hops plant as a vine that sprouts each April. Its blossoms turn into inch-long seed cones, similar to a hemlock cone, at the end of the growing season.

"The seeds were ground fine," writes Rose E. Eash, who remembered a hops plant on the Abraham Baer property next to the Quemahoning Dam. "I used the hop seed in the bread-baking yet in 1925. That was when the countrywomen saved the yeast from one baking to another. Every few months yeast was borrowed from the neighbor for a 'fresh start.' We did this until the '30s when we could buy fresh yeast cakes."

Not only did the most definitive information on hop snow come from elderly sources, but in most instances they cited someone elderly they knew while young as their source of information. Rose Eash, for example, learned about hops from an eighty-two-year-old woman whom she cared for in 1924. Also interesting was that most of those who knew of hop snow were German in ancestry—although not necessarily Pennsylvania Dutch; my Amish sources were not familiar with the term. Several were German Catholic. Others were Brethren (German Protestants of a different religious ancestry than Amish and Mennonites).

Hops are grown in Germany for beer brewing. Whether the phrase may have originated there is a possibility. However, given that national weather services and the *Old Farmer's Almanac* knew nothing of the term, I'm still betting this is a regionalized Pennsylvania-German phrase.

So if we get a snowfall later this month, call it a hop snow, think of fresh-baked bread and a heritage-phrase worth preserving.

First published in April 2005.

Winter Is a Gift For the Soul

As my years pile on one another, I will admit it's becoming harder to generate enthusiasm for winter and the shoveling and scraping and treacherous driving that keeps it company. During the recent spell of wet, dismal weather, I found myself saying, "At least it's not snow." Now that it's made a timely entrance for the holidays, however, I'm thawing to winter's inevitable presence and wondering at my unwelcoming attitude.

It's Christmastime! Be honest. Can you truly feel the exhilaration of that statement if the thermometer is hovering around forty and a steady drizzle is falling? People in other parts of the country celebrate the holidays with barbeques and walks in Bermudas on the beach. I've been in those places at this time and it's pleasant, but I prefer our holiday season.

Picture a Christmas Eve with eight inches of cotton-like snow dropping gently, piling perfectly, on roof and post and line. Decorative lights, just warm enough to carve little grottos into snowy banks, add patterns of bright color to the serene scene. The crisply cool evening air tastes as clean as filtered spring water. Everything is still, incredibly quiet. For the moment, you know soul-deep peace and spiritual refreshment.

Winter brings us contrasts: often harsh conditions outside create glowing memories inside. This is very much a part of our heritage. For eighteenth-century settlers, winter was a season to survive. They did so seated close to crackling fires and warmth-radiating hearths as the wind whistled through chinks between the logs and snow sifted in around shutters. Family togetherness was a requirement, imposed by the heat source. Sleighs brought people together for day-long church and family-centered holiday celebrations. Hot wassail or cider chased the bone-numbing chill of transit. The joy of company created the real warmth of the season. We call them "good old days" and believe our ancestors were more loving and neighborly. In truth, they had little choice. They could get along—or face the prospect of a long, cold, dark winter alone, beyond the hearth's glow or companionship's comfort.

Yet despite all of our contemporary conveniences, winter still compels us to find comfort in company. While our homes offer better shelter, we still treasure the fire, the warm drink and fellowship with others. While our vehicles are weather-tight and heated, we will scrape windshields and challenge treacherous roads or endure crowded airports and uncertain flight schedules to be with our loved ones. Without winter, would such experiences retain as much meaning?

The First Frontier

I probably have your agreement to much of this as it applies to the holidays. But most of us probably would wish winter away on January 2. So here's where I step off the shoveled path: remember the lessons of Christmastime and embrace the entire winter for its qualities, even as you cope with its difficulties.

For if the bitter season will be with us for months, so will its scenic beauty and almost celestial moments. Take the day in early March when I was driving north along U.S. Route 219 between Johnstown and Ebensburg, climbing up the Allegheny Ridge. The day was bright with sunshine, unimpeded by the scattered gauzy clouds. Freezing rain had coated hillsides of maple, oak and sumac. With the sun as high as it gets in the winter sky, I was being treated to a crystalline light show that only God himself can produce. At a distance, ice-coated trees became countless gossamer feather dusters, brushing the deep blue sky. The trees nearest to my vehicle seemed almost neon in intensity—crystal thickets collecting sunlight and then casting it from limb ends and tree tops like fiber-optic lamps. Stopping alongside the highway and stepping out of the car, I filled my lungs with the fresh ice-filtered air and spent a few moments witnessing the ephemeral display.

It is at such moments, whether on a March day or a Christmas Eve, that we can appreciate winter's beauty and spiritual qualities. At such a moment we can sense—deep within—that winter is another gift from God to experience.

First published in December 2004.

Many Names, One Place

Picture a majestic morning sky in late July: dapple-gray dumpling clouds hint at hidden sunlight as a thousand misty wisps twist upward from the hardwooded hills. Or remember the time you were traveling and just had to say "hello" to that group of strangers after overhearing one ask another, "Where were y'uns?" And when was the last time you went to a local festival or fair that *didn't* offer pierogies? All are familiar sights, sounds and tastes whether your home is in Altoona or Aliquippa, Windber or Washington.

We live in a special place. A place with a mixture of qualities and characteristics unique in all the world. We just don't know what to call it. Our geographic region ranges from southwestern Pennsylvania into south-

Pennsylvania's Allegheny Mountains

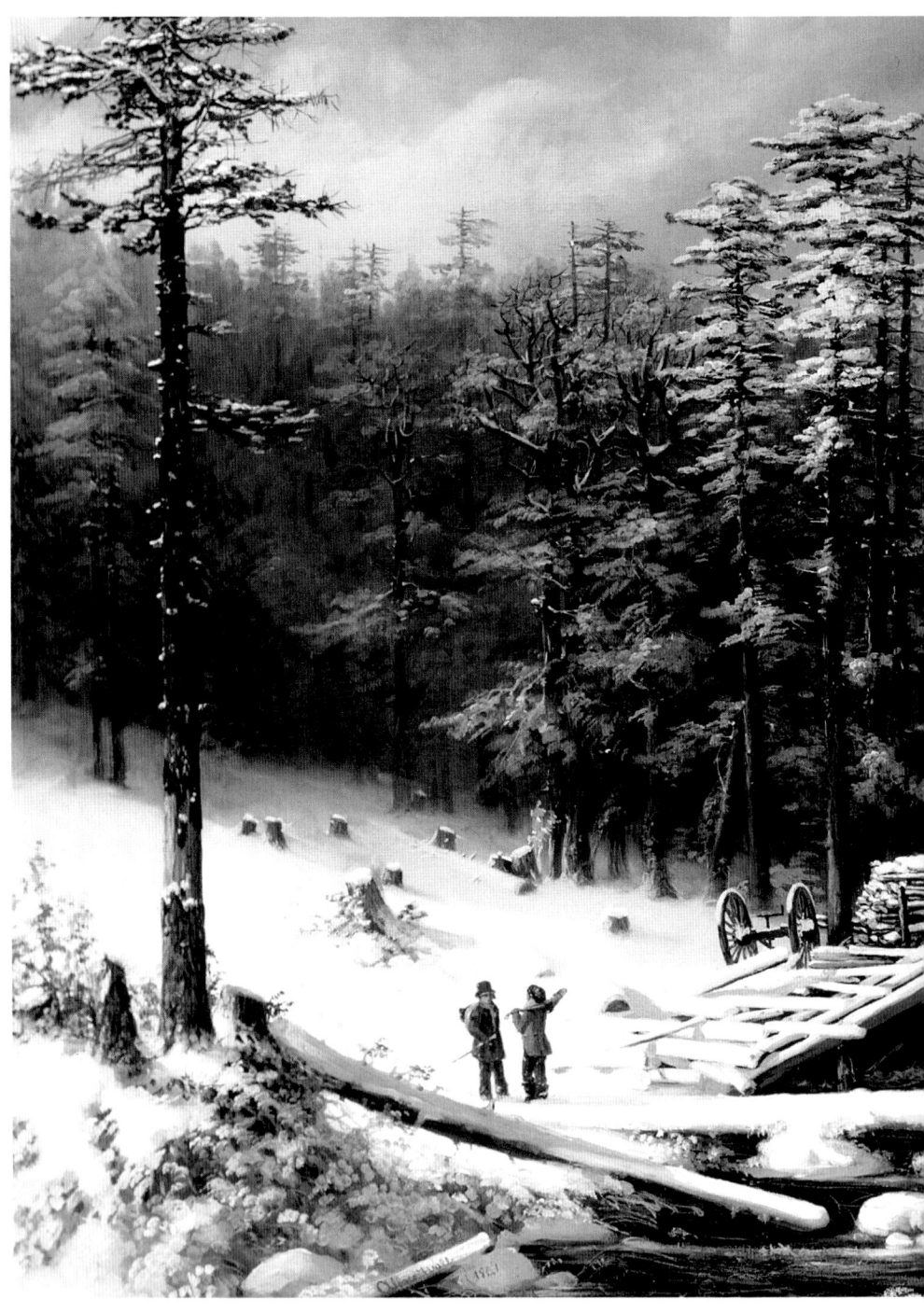

Old Saw Mill painted by Alfred Wall in the Allegheny Summit community of Lilly, 1851.
Westmoreland Museum of American Art, Greensburg, Pennsylvania. Gift of the Woods-Marchand Foundation.

The First Frontier

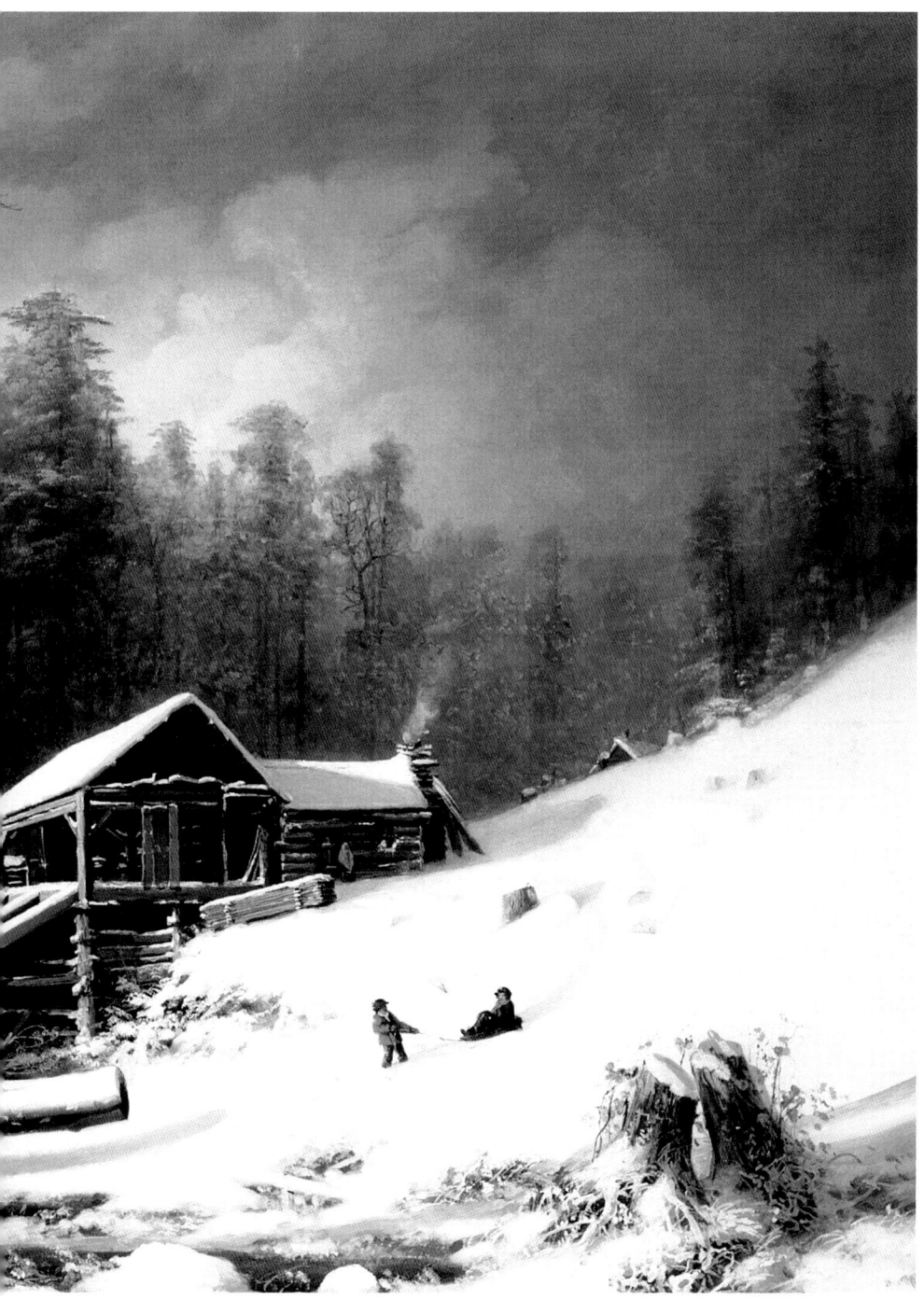

Pennsylvania's Allegheny Mountains

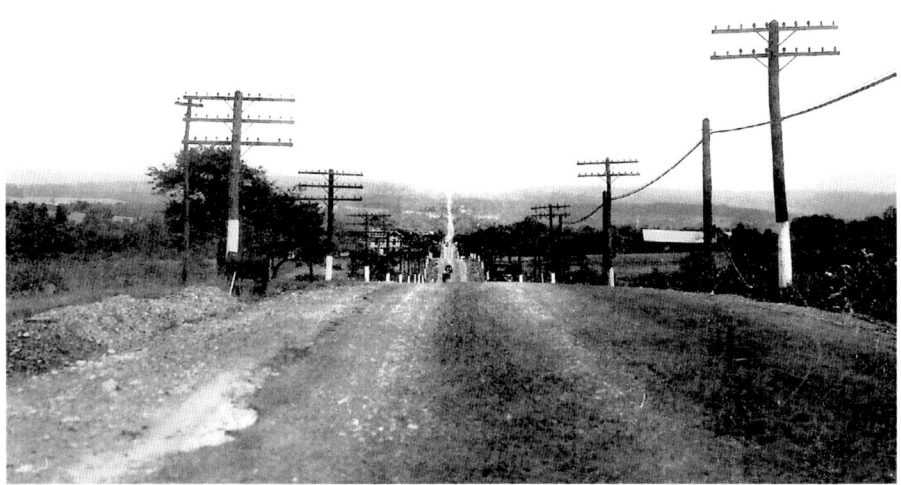

This was known as the "Seven Mile Stretch" of the Lincoln Highway across the Allegheny Plateau in Somerset County. *Lincoln Highway Heritage Corridor.*

central Pennsylvania. Much of it is called Pittsburgh or Steeler Country. Portions of it are known as the Alleghenies and the Laurel Highlands. All of these names fit. None of them, however, embraces our place.

More than $100 million federal and state dollars have been poured into the research and development of this region's heritage. "America's Industrial Heritage Project" was a mid-1980s effort by the National Park Service to identify and develop the qualities that make this region special. A Path of Progress National Heritage Route was created and then a Rivers of Steel National Heritage Area. The state established the Allegheny Ridge Heritage Area, the Lincoln Highway Heritage Corridor, the National Road Heritage Corridor and the Rivers of Steel Heritage Area (which is also a national heritage area).

One private nonprofit organization, created to define and present the region's heritage, discovered that frontiersmen gathered at Fort Pitt in 1776 and drafted a petition calling on the Continental Congress to establish a new territory called "Westsylvania." In a classic case of bad timing, the frontier petition was sent in July of that year; the Continental Congress was a bit preoccupied with declaring independence from the king of England, and the Westsylvania petition died in committee. Delighted with the discovery, however, the nonprofit group titled its magazine *Westsylvania* and renamed

The First Frontier

itself the Westsylvania Heritage Corporation. However, the Westsylvania of the original petition took in much more than our place—basically the entire Allegheny Mountain chain as far south, possibly, as the Cumberland Gap where Virginia, Kentucky and Tennessee meet.

Agencies responsible for marketing our place to visitors have not embraced the Westsylvania label. That's not surprising given that the state's tourism promotion program is a county-based system that makes any regional promotion a challenge. The result is advertising for the Allegheny Mountains, Armstrong County, Bedford County, Fulton County, Greater Johnstown/Cambria County, Greater Pittsburgh, Huntingdon County, Indiana County, the Laurel Highlands, Somerset County, the Alleghenies and Washington County.

What, then, do we call our place? After spending more than twenty years writing about regional-heritage tourism and countless hours deliberating and debating that issue with colleagues and coworkers, my conclusion is…it doesn't matter. Use whatever name you want. Just understand how your name fits within the larger context of our place. Take the Lincoln Highway Heritage Corridor—U.S. Route 30. Always scenic, often beautiful, it becomes more interesting when you look for remnants of its Lincoln Highway period. Experience its Forbes Road period at Fort Bedford, Fort Ligonier and Fort Pitt and the corridor becomes fascinating.

Think of all these names as rooms in a regional house. My goal is to bring you into new rooms and encourage you to explore the familiar ones with fresh eyes, to deepen our appreciation of the one name that means the most to all of us: "home."

First published in March 2003.

PART II

The People of the Alleghenies:

A Peak and Valley Melting Pot

The Alleghenies weren't the most inviting place to be in the eighteenth century—for natives or for Europeans. Lenape and Iroquois tribes lived here for a generation or two while being pushed westward by growing European settlement along the Atlantic coast. Initial European settlement came slowly, tentatively, until nineteenth-century transportation developments opened the region to easier travel and commerce. Then groups came in waves, one following the next, continually redefining who were the "haves" and the "have nots."

The stories of the Alleghenies' people are as dramatic as its vistas are scenic. These are tales of almost unimaginable labor, inspiring faith and heroic self-sacrifice. Reflecting the character of the place itself, the American dream was achieved here through grit, rocklike determination and erosive perseverance.

What We Say Reflects Who We Are

I have a favorite postcard that someone sent me. It's titled "The First Pittsburgher" and displays a cartoon scene of a solitary, bearskin-clad cave man holding a spear and standing at the point where the Allegheny and Monongahela Rivers come together to form the Ohio. There are palm trees along the banks, a volcano in the background and a pterodactyl in the sky overhead. This first Pittsburgher is saying just one word: "Yinz!"

"Yinz," "yunz," "y'uns"—we may be unsure how to spell it, and the dictionaries don't list it, but there isn't another word that better captures our region. Go anywhere in the country—in the world, for that matter—and if you hear someone say, "Are yunz going to the store?" you know that they're from somewhere in a little pocket of Appalachia comprised of south-central and southwestern Pennsylvania, southeastern Ohio, northern West Virginia and western Maryland.

A number of years ago, while launching a regional magazine as its editor, I wanted to use this word as the heading for the letters-to-the-editor section—but how to spell it? That question led to some research. You may be aware that our word has the same linguistic roots as the South's "y'all," the East Coast's "youse" and the ubiquitous "you guys." We seem to have an innate need for a specific second-person-plural pronoun—and American English doesn't provide one. Old English did, according to *The American Heritage Dictionary of the English Language*. Back in the thirteenth century, if speaking to one person, you would refer to "thee"; if addressing more than one, you said "you." By the eighteenth century, usage had narrowed to "you" for both singular and plural second-person references.

One of this country's most significant groups of early immigrants—the Scots-Irish (also known as the Ulster English)—brought a Gaelic plural "yous" with them when they settled among the Appalachian Mountains, the eighteenth century's western frontier. "Yous" evolved into "you-all" in the South and, over time, became "y'all." To the northeast, it became "youse." In our region it evolved from "you-ones" to "you-uns" to "y'uns." This is the spelling I settled on for the magazine's letters-to-the-editor section and the spelling that—I believe—is proper for this improper word.

Is "y'uns" truly so improper, though? Readers had an enjoyable debate about that in the early issues of the magazine. Some felt that its usage is a sign of poor education, others—among whom I count myself—consider it a distinctive badge of our heritage. The Scots-Irish were considered coarse, uneducated and ill-mannered by the mostly English residents of the "civilized" eighteenth-century eastern seaboard. Isn't it interesting how colloquial words and phrases, originating with the Scots-Irish, carry a similar connotation today?

As a writer, I know the importance of proper vocabulary, grammar and syntax. They are tools of my trade. But as a heritage writer, I also appreciate the way our unique words and phrases enrich our lives and reflect who we are. Yes, I can spell "hiking," but I can still say I'm going hikin'. I can

The First Frontier

write about our slippery winter roads yet caution someone to be careful walking because the sidewalks are "slippy." And I can smile when hearing an Allegheny Mountain mother call after her kids, "Y'uns be careful!" These are priceless heirlooms of our Scots-Irish heritage, as rooted in our region as the hardwoods are on our ridges. Don't say "y'uns" if you don't want to—just embrace it as part of who we are.

I find myself reflecting on this while away from home on extended business in the land of "y'all," where I'm hearing the rich inflections and colorful speech patterns of the Deep South and the Cajun. While writing these words, the realization struck me: I miss y'uns.

First published in November 2005.

Honoring the Scots-Irish

Many's the year when I've toasted Saint Patrick and wished that my surname started with "O'," or maybe with "Mac" since I feel similarly about the Scots. Celtic blood courses through me. While Hurst is an English name, other branches of my family tree belong to Johnstons and Reeds, who were among those ethnic mongrels known as Scots-Irish. At least "ethnic mongrels" approximated my ancestral feelings until recently, when I read *Born Fighting: How the Scots-Irish Shaped America*, a book by James Webb that proudly delineates this ethnic group and extols its impact on our nation.

These are the people who arguably founded our region. In describing them, Webb explains much of the independent spirit, fragmentation and ornery stubbornness that characterizes the people of Pennsylvania's Allegheny Mountains to this day. Webb has impressive credentials. Elected to the United States Senate in 2006, he was a decorated marine veteran of Vietnam who also served as secretary of the navy during the Reagan administration. As a writer, he has six novels, including *Fields of Fire*, and a film, *Rules of Engagement*, to his credit.

In *Born Fighting*, the author traces the evolution of the Scots-Irish from the group's Celtic roots through its origins in the lowlands of Scotland, its development in the "Ulster Plantation" of Northern Ireland and its immigration to America in the 1700s and early 1800s. He defines the Scots-Irish less by nationality than by familial connections and shared cultural characteristics: They were hard-edged and disciplined yet sensual, lacking

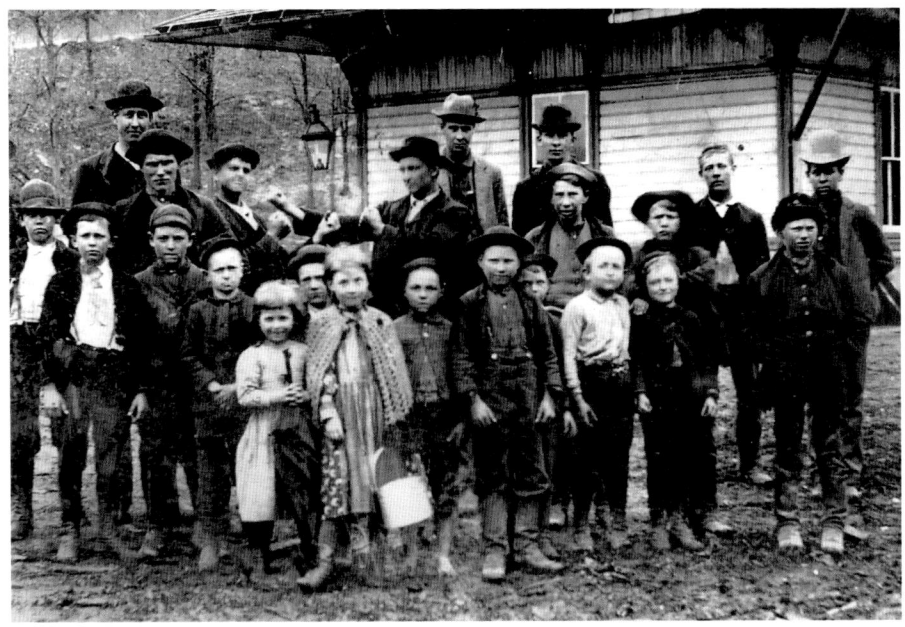

Fayette County mountain folk pose in front of the Ohiopyle train station circa 1920. *Coal and Coke Heritage Center, Pennsylvania State University–Fayette, Eberly Campus, Mitchell Collection.*

in education but possessing practical intellect, difficult to govern but reliable and loyal to leaders who earned their respect.

"Many of these families had spent more than a hundred years in Ireland," writes Webb. "Almost all had spent more than a generation there, so that their children had no direct memory of Scotland. Some observers claim that they were at this point neither Scottish nor Irish. The truth is that they were both, having gleaned from the culture of one people and the land of another until they were a unique hybrid mix."

In the Scottish lowlands, these hardy people subsisted on farming and warfare. They were the people of William Wallace (depicted in *Braveheart*), fighting alternately the English and one another, trusting in clan and family, honing military skills, refining their sense of egalitarianism and resisting any authority with which they disagreed. When they converted from Catholicism, it was not to Anglicanism but to Calvinism, with its bottom-up governmental structure based on the Kirk (the Presbyterian Church of Scotland). And it was more their struggle with Anglicanism than with Catholicism that drove them in successive waves from Scotland to Ulster to America. Most of them washed through Philadelphia toward the western frontier—the Appalachian

The First Frontier

Mountains of Pennsylvania, Virginia and the Carolinas—where they could live on their own terms. There the Scots-Irish subsisted once again on farming and warfare, fighting alternately with the natives, the French and the British, trusting in extended family, using their ingrained military skills, spreading their populist Democracy and mistrusting most authority.

While Webb's narrative follows the movement of his people southward, he would have no trouble trailing the Scots-Irish in our region. They squatted on land here before it was opened for settlement and then formed many of our earliest communities, including Pittsburgh. Westsylvania's history of confrontations with Indians, the French, the British, the governments of Pennsylvania and Virginia and even our own federal government during the Whiskey Rebellion all involved Scots-Irish. Today, their influence lingers here in our largely conservative values, centered on home and family and patriotism, our manner of speech ("y'uns") and our insistence on the smallest levels of government (which at least partially explains our multiplicity of municipalities).

So if the Irish have Saint Patrick's Day, and the Scots have Robert Burns's celebrations, shouldn't the Scots-Irish have a day? (I can hear my ancestors now: "Why doesn't the ninny just pick a day and be done with it? Must be the English in him.")

First published in March 2006.

Happy Saint David's Day

As we drag through these dark days of winter, take heart. It's time to celebrate a saint's day. Saint Patrick? Well, yes, him too, but I'm talking about Saint David! So put a leek in your cap and get ready for Dydd Dewi Sant at the nearest Gymanfa Ganu—what's that? What am I talking about? And what happened to my vowels?

Dydd Dewi Sant—Saint David's Day—is the national day of Wales, and it falls on March 1 each year. The leek is Wales' national symbol, and on this day good Welshmen and Welshwomen put leeks in their caps (daffodils also are acceptable) and celebrate with choral music festivals called Gymanfa Ganu. Saint David is Wales' patron saint, a Welsh priest and bishop who founded a dozen or more monasteries in Wales and England during the sixth century. He and his monks lived highly disciplined lives, pulling their own

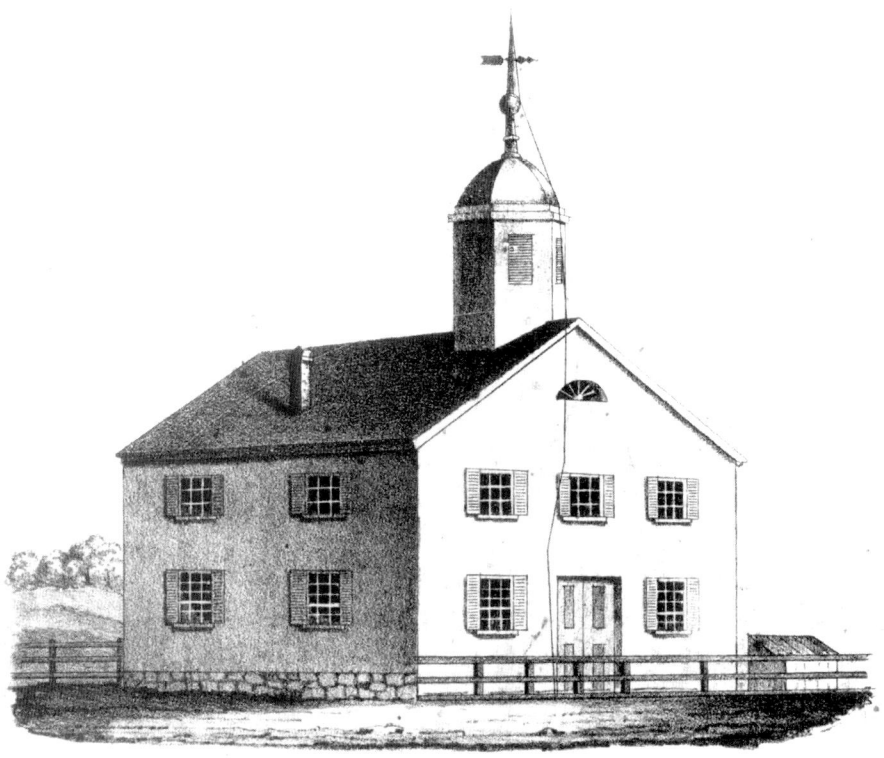

Illustration from an 1854 map of the Welsh church in Ebensburg, the largest in the United States in the mid-nineteenth century. *Cambria County Historical Society.*

plows, eating no meat and drinking only water. While leeks have a place in Welsh tradition going back to the ancient days of the Druids, their honored status stems from a battle between Saint David's men and pagan Saxon invaders, in which David ordered his soldiers to fix leeks to their helmets as a way to distinguish them from their enemy.

So what does this have to do with us? If your family is long-established in this region, Welsh blood may flow through your veins (as it does through mine). And if you count coal miners, iron makers, quarrymen and steelworkers among family members, you share a common industrial heritage. Seeking religious freedom, Welsh Quakers, Baptists and Calvinists came to William Penn's colony in the late seventeenth century and actually accounted for one-third of Pennsylvania's population circa 1700. If you ever wondered about the odd names of Philadelphia-area communities such as Bala-Cynwyd and Bryn Mawr, now you know their roots. A second wave of Welsh arrived in

The First Frontier

the late eighteenth and nineteenth centuries, and many of them came to Westsylvania before fanning across the country. Welsh families settled on the high plateau of the Alleghenies, establishing Ebensburg and a county that they named "Cambria," after a mountainous region in their homeland. During much of the nineteenth century, Ebensburg was a jumping-off point for many immigrating Welsh starting new lives in the United States. At the time of the Civil War, the largest Welsh Congregational Church in the United States was located in Ebensburg.

Because the Industrial Revolution occurred fifty years earlier in Wales than in the United States, many of the Welsh came with skills in great demand here and figured prominently in the early developments within our region. Northern Cambria and Indiana counties still are dotted with coal-mining communities founded by the Welsh, including Griffithtown and Nanty Glo. "Nant y glo" is Welsh for "streams of coal." Welsh cut the nine-hundred-foot Staple Bend Tunnel for the Allegheny Portage Railroad in the 1830s—the first railroad tunnel in the United States. They were puddlers in the first iron furnaces and rollers in the first integrated mills. Others were coal miners, quarrymen and tin platers. Their skills kept some employed in Cambria County mines and mills, while others moved on to Pittsburgh, Ohio and other points west. By the time central and southern European immigrants began arriving in the late 1800s, the Welsh had fanned across our region and were already considered part of the social establishment.

Since the Welsh were among the earliest immigrants and never came in massive numbers, they tended to assimilate into Anglo-Saxon America fairly quickly. Yet ripples of Welsh heritage remain. Two United Church of Christ churches in Ebensburg preserve their Welsh roots by commemorating Saint David's Day on the first Sunday after March 1 each year by singing Welsh hymns and placing daffodils and leeks on the altar. There is a Saint David's Society of Pittsburgh and a Welsh Nationality Room in the Cathedral of Learning at the University of Pittsburgh.

So we should celebrate Saint David's Day. If you'd rather wait for Saint Patrick's Day, consider this: Some historians believe that Saint Patrick was actually a Welshman named Maewyn Succat. Try toasting that name after a bit o' green beer.

First published in February 2007.

Celebrate the Irish—For the Right Reasons

When the green beer's flowing, the band is playing a jig and buttons blossom that say "Kiss me, I'm Irish," it is easy to forget that there was a time when the sons of Saint Patrick weren't welcome here, a time when the Irish were a minority group working the hardest, dirtiest, most dangerous jobs; living in substandard conditions; and suffering religious and social discrimination. Sadly, that was as true within our region as it was in Boston and New York City. If New York City had its street gangs and Five Points slums, we had constant brawling anywhere Irish laborers were working at the time and Irish millworker neighborhoods with names such as "Rotten Row." Yet the Irish play important roles in our most dramatic stories: the Pennsylvania Main Line Canal, the Pennsylvania Railroad, iron and steelmaking, coal mining, unionization, religious tolerance, Americanization and, ultimately, celebration of diversity.

If we describe the initial Europeans to come here—English, Germans, Scots-Irish and Welsh—as "settlers" or "founding fathers," then the Irish were our first immigrants. Scots-Irish were predominantly lowland Scots in ancestry, who came to America after spending a generation or two in Ulster (Northern Ireland). They were overwhelmingly Protestant—as were most of the other first settlers. These farmers, craftspeople and traders formed the first social establishment.

A few Catholic Irish found their way to our region in those earliest days. Unity Township in Westmoreland County, for example, had a sufficient number of German and Irish Catholics in 1789 to require a resident priest. Their meeting place eventually became the site of Saint Vincent College. Father Demetrius Gallitzin came to an Irish settlement of ten families on the Allegheny Summit in the late 1790s, adopted the community and gave it the name "Loretto." Fifty years later, six Franciscan religious brothers—also Irish—founded an academy there that is Saint Francis University today. Irish laborers dug the Main Line Canal circa 1830, receiving from seventy-five to eighty-seven cents for a twelve-hour workday and enduring living conditions that bred malaria, typhoid and cholera. Writings of the period described these Irish as "largely illiterate, Roman Catholic and full of the brogue," compared to the now-established Protestant Scots-Irish who were "hardy and sober citizens who recognized the value of education."

Until the potato famine of the 1840s, Irish immigration had occurred in the form of a steady trickle of men. However, the fungus that destroyed Ireland's potato crops drove entire families—a half-million people over the decade—to

The First Frontier

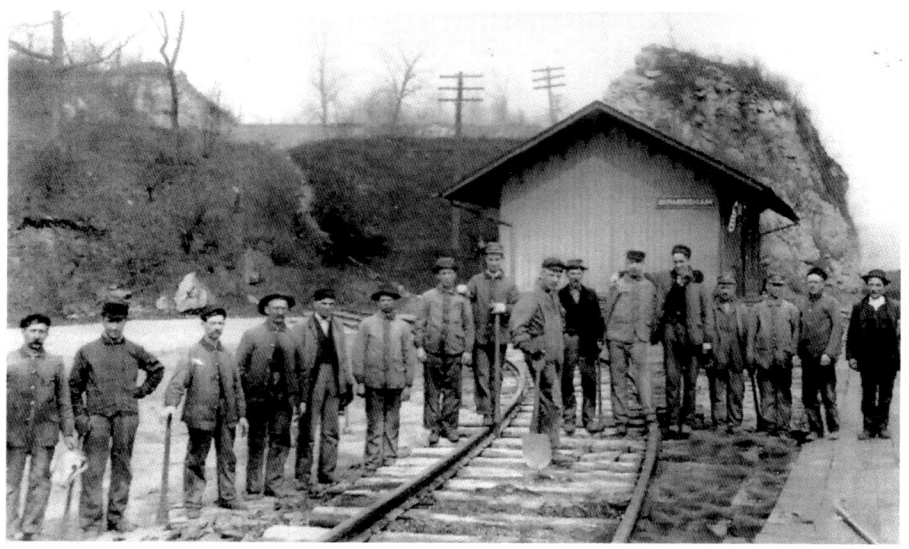

Limestone quarry workers in West Birmingham, known locally as "Irish Flats." *Tyrone Area Historical Society.*

American shores. The Pennsylvania Railroad imported Irish workers in the 1850s to lay track and build the Horseshoe Curve, an engineering landmark still in use today. Irish millworkers' families comprised the majority of two residential sections of Greater Johnstown in 1870, including neighborhoods that were clearly substandard, according to the records of the day. Irish also mined coal and were active in some of the earliest unionization efforts. By the time of the 1880 census, more than 236,000 Irish lived in Pennsylvania—5.5 percent of the population. Within a generation, many of them here had moved up in status, and new waves of emigrants from central, eastern and southern Europe were replacing the Irish at the bottom of America's social order. However, Irish religious discrimination persisted well into the twentieth century. Saint Francis College, for example, struggled with anti-Catholic politics for almost ten years before finally obtaining a charter from the state in 1921.

So on that annual day when most of us manage to find at least a wee bit of Irish blood running through our veins, celebrate, certainly, but lift your first glass to Irish accomplishments within our region, Irish perseverance amid adversity and Irish enrichment of our culture. Then lift your second to all of the immigrant groups who have followed their example ever since.

First published in March 2009.

Pennsylvania's Allegheny Mountains

Underground Railroad Stories Are Surfacing

If you were to pick one adjective that captures the personality of our region, "contentious" would be a good candidate. Consider the Native Americans we chased out; George Washington leading an army here to deal with our whiskey boys; Andrew Carnegie and Henry Clay Frick literally battling our millworkers; and our union coalminers, who traditionally have fought with one another only slightly less than they have with mine operators.

During the turbulent period leading up to the Civil War, this region must have been a caldron of contentiousness—on both sides of the great debates of the day. Some of our residents strongly supported the supremacy of states' rights over federal, and we tend to forget that there were slaveholders here—as well as ardent abolitionists. All of this made Pennsylvania's Allegheny Mountains a rather hazardous place for escaped slaves, Underground Railroad conductors, slave hunters and U.S. marshals alike. Whether people were freeing slaves or tracking them, they had to exercise extreme caution.

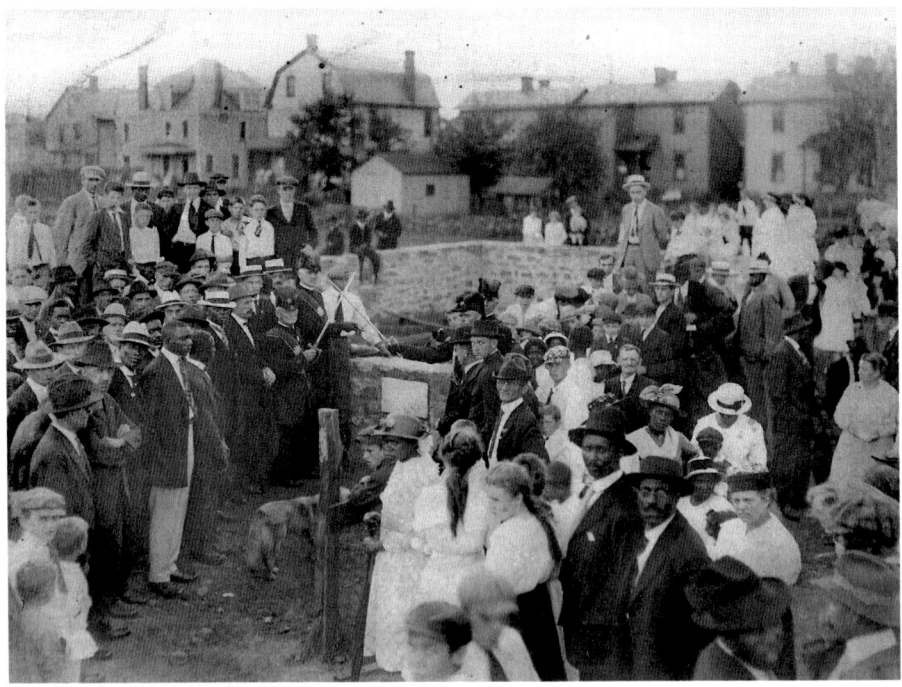

Cornerstone-setting ceremony about 1917 for the Second Baptist Church of Blairsville, now the Underground Railroad Museum. *Historical Society of the Blairsville Area.*

The First Frontier

Perhaps that's why so little is known about Underground Railroad activity here, compared to central and eastern Pennsylvania, where one can find more abundant histories and interpretations of them at visitor sites and museums. Slowly, however, some of our communities are learning more about this dramatic time in their history—and beginning to present their stories in ways that offer new, interesting experiences for us.

The LeMoyne House in Washington, Pennsylvania, is the state's first national historic landmark of the Underground Railroad, interpreting the life of Dr. Francis Julius LeMoyne, who used his own home and other properties to help runaway slaves make their way to safety. Local historians believe that the Indiana County community of Blairsville was an important Underground Railroad station that processed thousands of escaped slaves on their way north along a corridor that roughly paralleled U.S. Route 119. They have developed an Underground Railroad–themed walking tour, reenactments of an 1858 slave rescue, a special website and a Blairsville Underground Railroad Museum. Meanwhile, other Indiana County researchers have tied Underground Railroad and abolitionist activity to several buildings in downtown Indiana. They also have found U.S. Circuit Court documents from the 1847 trial of Dr. Robert Mitchell of Diamondville near Clymer, who was accused of harboring and concealing a fugitive slave.

Juneteenth is celebrated each year in Bedford: an annual, national observance commemorating the end of slavery in the United States, an event that emphasizes reflection, education and multicultural celebration. The name was derived from its date of origin: June 19, 1865, the day that slaves in Galveston, Texas, learned that they were free. Their celebration turned into an annual event that, 141 years later, continues to spread across the country.

Researchers have discovered a variety of other interesting stories involving African Americans within the Alleghenies. There's Edinborough Smith, a slave turned teamster in the Continental army who was at Yorktown when the British surrendered to George Washington. Smith, who married into a family that had settled atop Laurel Hill, was murdered in 1865. Samuel Williams, a Johnstown barber, organized a group of African American families from neighboring Pennsylvania Main Line Canal communities to go to Liberia in 1853. William Nesbit, a Hollidaysburg barber, was a co-organizer but didn't like Liberia. He returned and wrote a critical book titled *Four Months in Liberia*. Williams remained and wrote a positive book in response to Nesbit's, titled *Four Years in Liberia*. Then, during the Civil

War, Nesbit's son, William "Wilbur" Nesbit, and ten other young black men from Hollidaysburg, Altoona and Huntingdon joined the famed Fifty-fourth Massachusetts Infantry—one of the first colored regiments to fight for the Union.

Learning more about African American heritage in Pennsylvania's Alleghenies is an opportunity for people of all ethnic backgrounds to learn more about themselves, to explore their diversity and influences on one another. We might even discover some reasons why being contentious can be a good thing.

First published in June 2006.

Faith Can Save Cambria City Churches

From Ireland, the Ukraine, Germany, Poland, Hungary, Croatia, Ruthenia, Serbia, Slovakia, Italy and Greece they came, entering the twentieth century and new lives through Ellis Island. These immigrants—mostly men from rural, Old World villages—were snagged by Cambria Steel Company recruiters and put on trains to Johnstown. While necessary as unskilled laborers for Cambria's mills and coal mines, many of these immigrants were scorned by Johnstowners as unwashed "Hungarians." They were given the hardest, most dangerous jobs, paid a pittance and relegated to the suburb closest to the mill: Cambria City. Most of these men planned to earn money and return to their homeland and families. Whether by happenstance or design, though, many stayed and either brought their families over or started families here.

Because they were shunned by the greater community, the immigrants' new world was Cambria City. They packed into tiny wood-framed houses, gardened and raised livestock in postage stamp–sized yards, shopped with what little money they had in neighborhood stores and worshipped in neighborhood churches. And the church was central in their lives. God gave them the faith to endure. Their children were educated in parochial schools. What social lives they enjoyed were spent with their own kind at church functions and in ethnic clubs.

The important role that religion played in these immigrants' lives can be seen today. In a neighborhood that is now only three blocks wide and ten blocks long (half of Cambria City was lost to urban renewal

The First Frontier

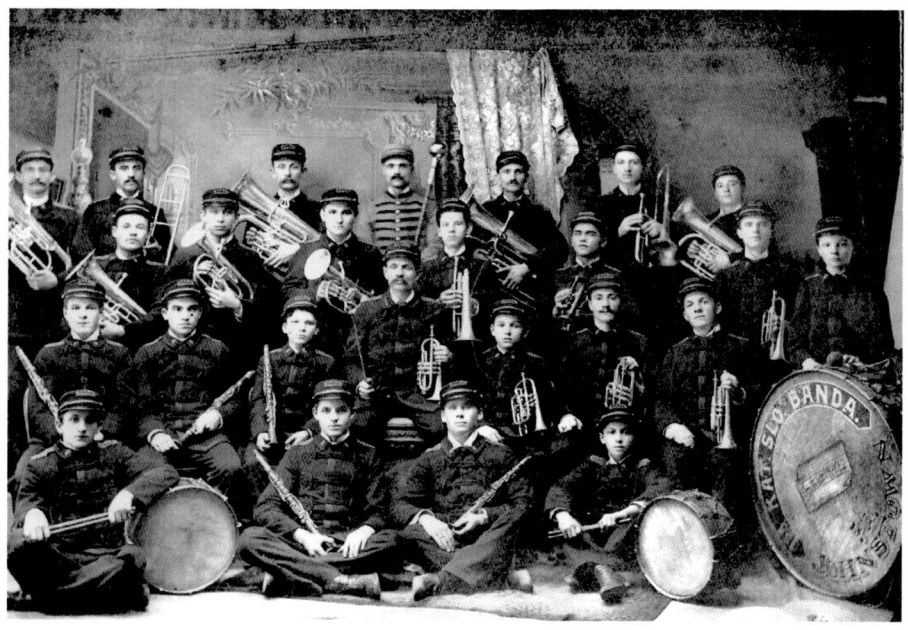

The First Catholic Slovak Band in Cambria City around the turn of the twentieth century. *Johnstown Area Heritage Association.*

in the 1960s), there are still nine churches—all of them founded by ethnic groups and built between 1901 and 1922. Gaze at their inspiring Romanesque towers, cathedral ceilings, stained glass, domes and statuary and then consider: these churches were built by men who worked eighty-four hours a week at the mill (for which they earned less than ten dollars) and by women who raised families and made extra money by caring for boarders in homes with about seven hundred square feet of living space. The churches of Cambria City are more than houses of worship. They are the embodiment of our region—and monuments to the religious faith, hard work and resolve that helped to make our nation a world power. That's why they sit at the heart of the Cambria City Historic District, listed on the National Register of Historic Places.

However, the realities of twenty-first-century societal trends don't make exceptions for ethnic icons. Because of dwindling numbers, finances and the lack of priests, in 2009 the Diocese of Altoona-Johnstown closed Immaculate Conception, originally a German parish; SS Casimir and Emerich, an already merged parish that had ministered to Hungarians and Poles; and St. Columba, whose parishioners were Italian and Irish.

The diocese merged them with St. Rochus, traditionally a Croatian parish, and St. Stephens, a Slovak church.

Are these historical landmarks, these cultural symbols of spiritual faith and American spirit, doomed to demolition? No. Many churches have been "retired" yet remain in use on a limited basis—often maintained and operated by some sort of not-for-profit entity, incorporated for that purpose. They open for special worship services, weddings, reenactments and other events. They can be given new life by being used for other purposes, such as becoming centers for performing arts or fine arts. Cambria City's concentration of churches poses both challenges and opportunities. Some sort of association, embracing all of the neighborhood's stakeholders, could work with the diocese or assume ownership of the properties if necessary. Business planning could devise strategies for the preservation and limited reuse of these churches. Outbuildings could be sold or rented, contributions could be solicited, special events and activities held—with the proceeds placed in a managed endowment for the perpetual care of the churches.

Might there be a national market for packaged ethnic weddings? Would visitors pay for guided tours given by costumed docents? Could special ethnic weekends, filled with worship, music, food and dancing, draw crowds? Perhaps the diocese or a religious order could organize an annual processional observance such as the Feast of Corpus Christi, featuring stops at all of the churches, that could draw hundreds or even thousands—with participants' gifts going into the perpetual care fund.

Consider that these churches were built by men working twelve-hour days in the mill and paid for from their earnings of twelve cents an hour. Somehow, women caring for families and boarders in four small rooms also found time to care for these churches and provide food for social functions. It won't be easy to save these churches, but it can be done—if we share our ancestors' faith and willingness to work.

First published in March 2008.

PART III

When the Alleghenies Were Wilderness

World War, Whiskey Boys and George Washington

It would be almost impossible to overstate the presence of Pennsylvania's Allegheny Mountains in early American history. They formed part of our first frontier, a mystical land of bountiful resources but immense obstacles, populated by fearsome natives. This is where a world war began and key battles determined that we would speak English rather than French. George Washington began his military career here—and a love-loathe relationship with this region that would bring him back both as a landowner and a conquering general. Native and new Americans traded brutalities amid these ridges. The commonwealths of Pennsylvania and Virginia both claimed this land, settlers petitioned to establish a new state instead and rebelling subsistence farmers here tested the fledgling United States' new federal government.

Yes, Pennsylvania's Alleghenies formed a major stage on which much of early America's most dramatic scenes were played. Yet 250 years later, there is a surprising array of ways to experience this legendary period. So, I'll take the point. We'll advance as a column in fire teams of two. Be watchful; keep your rifle at half-cock and your powder dry.

Hawkeye Was Here

It's too bad that James Fenimore Cooper didn't know what he was writing about. Had he, the setting for *The Last of the Mohicans* would have been

Pennsylvania's Allegheny Mountains

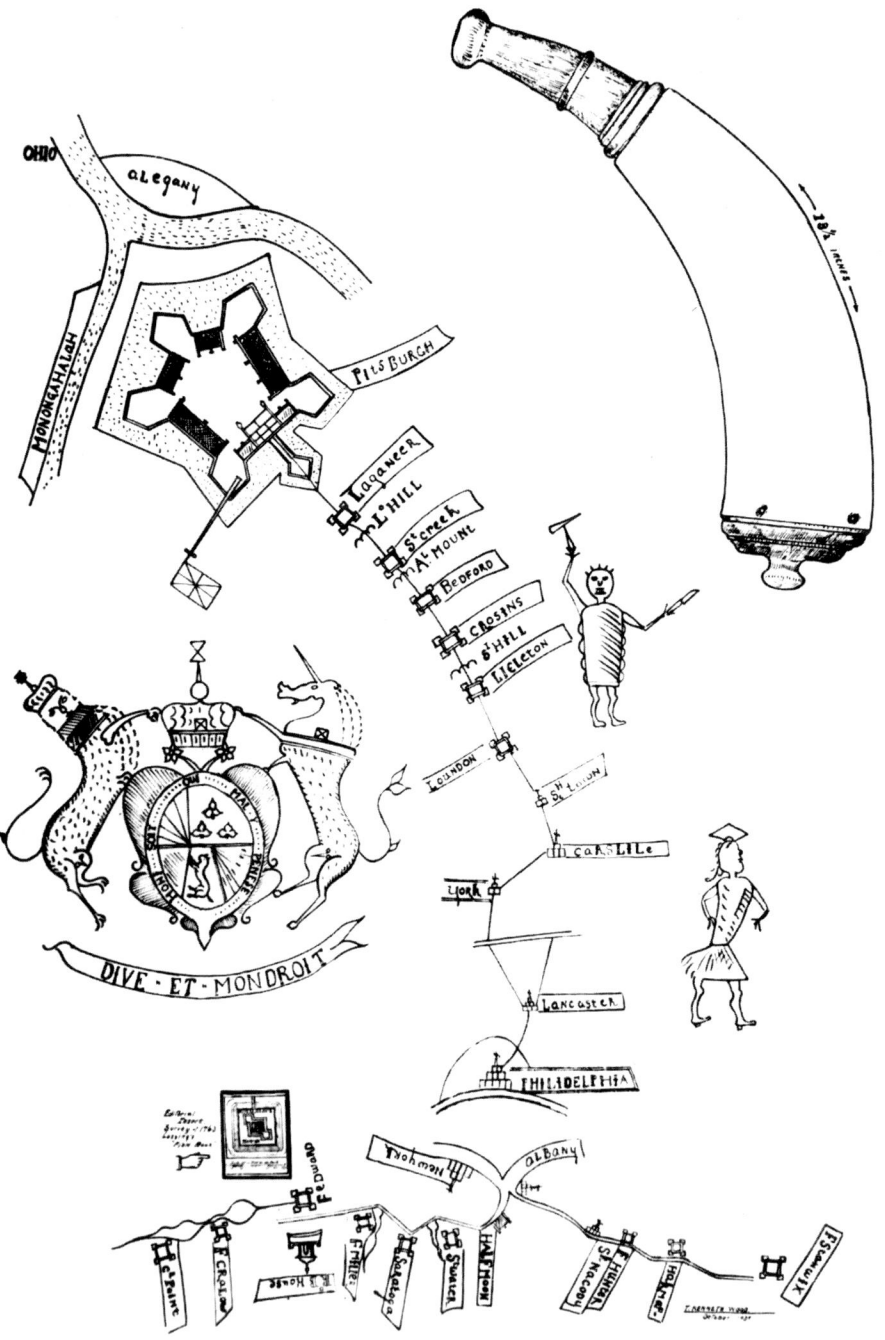

A copy of engravings on the powderhorn of French and Indian War veteran William Irvine. *Centre County Library and Historical Museum, Bellefonte, Pennsylvania.*

The First Frontier

southwestern Pennsylvania. The upper Ohio valley saw more action during the French and Indian War than the upper Hudson valley. Fort Duquesne was more of an epicenter than Fort William Henry. Frontiersman Christopher Gist was a real-life Hawkeye. And Cooper's hated Mingo lived here—not in upstate New York. (They were also not as black as Cooper painted them. They actually lived among the Delaware and Shawnee—their sworn enemies according to Cooper—and were basically neutral during the war.)

My purpose is not to beat on Mr. Cooper's fiction but to make a point: our region was a place of international focus, incredible tension and unquestionable danger during the period from 1754 to 1763. Without the slightest exaggeration or indulgence in hyperbole, this was the stuff of legends and epics. Consider how CNN would have covered this action 250 years ago.

On April 18, 1754, Fort Prince George, which just had been constructed at the Forks of the Ohio by a small Virginia militia, was seized by the French. The French immediately enlarged the fort and renamed it Fort Duquesne. Just a little more than a month later on May 28, 1754, a young, ambitious lieutenant colonel in Virginia's provincial militia by the name of George Washington—eager to impress the British—led a small force of forty Virginians and eleven Indians (including Mingo) to ambush a French encampment. In the firefight, the French commander was killed. The place still carries his name: Jumonville. Fearful of French reprisals, Washington and his men hastily erected a "fort of necessity." The Indians thought that Washington's position was defenseless and left. On July 3, 1754, the French and their Indian allies attacked Fort Necessity in a heavy rain and killed or wounded a third of Washington's men. The next day—July 4 of all days—Washington surrendered and was permitted to retreat by the gentlemanly French.

The French and Indian War was underway. Eventually, conflict would spread to Canada, the Caribbean, Europe, Africa, India, Singapore and the Philippines and would become known everywhere else as the Seven Years' War.

"So this was really the first world war," noted Martin West, director of Fort Ligonier. "The dispute [here] was over who would control access to the Ohio River."

That dispute would involve British, French and native and provincial forces here in Pennsylvania's Alleghenies for four years. The British would suffer an ignominious defeat when General Edward Braddock's forces were mauled at the Battle of the Monongahela one year later on July 9, 1755—during this action, Washington distinguished himself and began rebuilding his military career. General John Forbes's expeditionary force would ultimately be successful in regaining control of the Forks of the Ohio for the British in November 1758. And Colonel Henry Bouquet with a combined British/provincial force would deliver Fort Pitt from capture by Indians during the Battle of Bushy Run in August 1763.

Bushy Run Battlefield, a state historical site, is one of several places where you can experience the excitement and drama of that epochal time in American history today. Fort Ligonier is a recreation of the fortification, erected along Loyalhanna Creek during the French and Indian War, and offers an extensive collection of eighteenth-century artifacts, paintings and what may be the most complete set of recreated but period-authentic artillery pieces that exists anywhere in the nation. The Heinz History Center in Pittsburgh features a permanent exhibit, titled "Clash of Empires," that offers a comprehensive look at the Seven Years' War. Fort Pitt Museum is a state-operated museum at Point State Park in Pittsburgh. Fort Necessity National Battlefield near Farmington, operated by the National Park Service, interprets the war's earliest days and the site of George Washington's only military surrender.

Cooper could have based all of the Leatherstocking Tales in southwestern Pennsylvania—which reminds me that there's one other little detail that he got wrong. The Mohicans aren't extinct. Today, they're known as Stockbridge Indians and are alive and well in Wisconsin.

First published in March 2004.

Kittanning Trail Comes Alive

Although dawn's rays lit the Allegheny ridge top, it would be hours before the light of day would touch this deep defile hundreds of feet below. The dimness, morning mists and solemn chatter of Kittanning Creek all conspired to create a sense of wary excitement among the men of Armstrong Battalion, Pennsylvania Provincial Regiment. Moving in fire teams of two, signaling with gestures and whistled birdcalls, the column moved cautiously, quietly, from one side of the small stream to the other, working their way steadily up the Kittanning Pass. At a parley the previous evening, their chief scout,

The First Frontier

Lane Savage, had brought word of an Indian raiding party sighted along the trail somewhere ahead. Lieutenant Colonel John Armstrong had ordered his men to pack extra cartridges, and now they walked with their flintlock frizzens primed with black powder, their hammers at half-cock and all of their senses alert for a telltale sight, sound or scent signaling ambush.

For the 307 men of Armstrong Battalion in early September 1756, the 126-mile march from Fort Shirley near present-day Shirleysburg in Huntingdon County to the Delaware Indian village of Kit-han-ne—present-day Kittanning—must have been an incredibly nerve-wracking experience. They were chasing Indian raiders with European captives along the most used native path over the Alleghenies and through virgin forests of chestnut and hemlock that offered ever-present cover for surprise attacks.

The Delaware and related tribes had grown tired of being pushed off their ancestral lands into the continent's interior and were pushing back. Roving bands of warriors attacked isolated frontier homesteads, killed the men and took women and children back to their villages. British authorities were more concerned with French activities than with the Indians, whose actions were primarily affecting the provincials. Fear reigned on the frontier.

Armstrong's raid on Kit-han-ne marked the first time that settlers took the fight to the Indians and was considered a moral victory if not a tactical one. A chieftain, Captain Jacobs, was among the nine Delaware killed. The village was burned, and the Delaware were forced to abandon it. Armstrong's losses were seventeen killed, thirteen wounded and nineteen missing. Only a portion of the captives were freed. Still, Armstrong was hailed a hero by colonial America. The City of Philadelphia had a medal struck in his honor and gave one to each member of his command. Some historians believe this was the first American military medal ever awarded.

About 244 years later, a small column of eight reenactors replicated the Armstrong Expedition. With the exception of contemporary footwear (they tore up their feet trying to use moccasins the first day), the men were clothed, armed and outfitted in eighteenth-century fashion. They departed from the same place on the same day and walked all of the 126-mile trail corridor that they could locate, keeping to the original expedition's schedule and arriving in Kittanning on the September 8 anniversary of the battle. In most places, they had to walk along highways. But the day they hiked along Kittanning Creek up the Allegheny Front to Gallitzin, they knew they were treading the original Kittanning Trail. That knowledge, coupled with

Pennsylvania's Allegheny Mountains

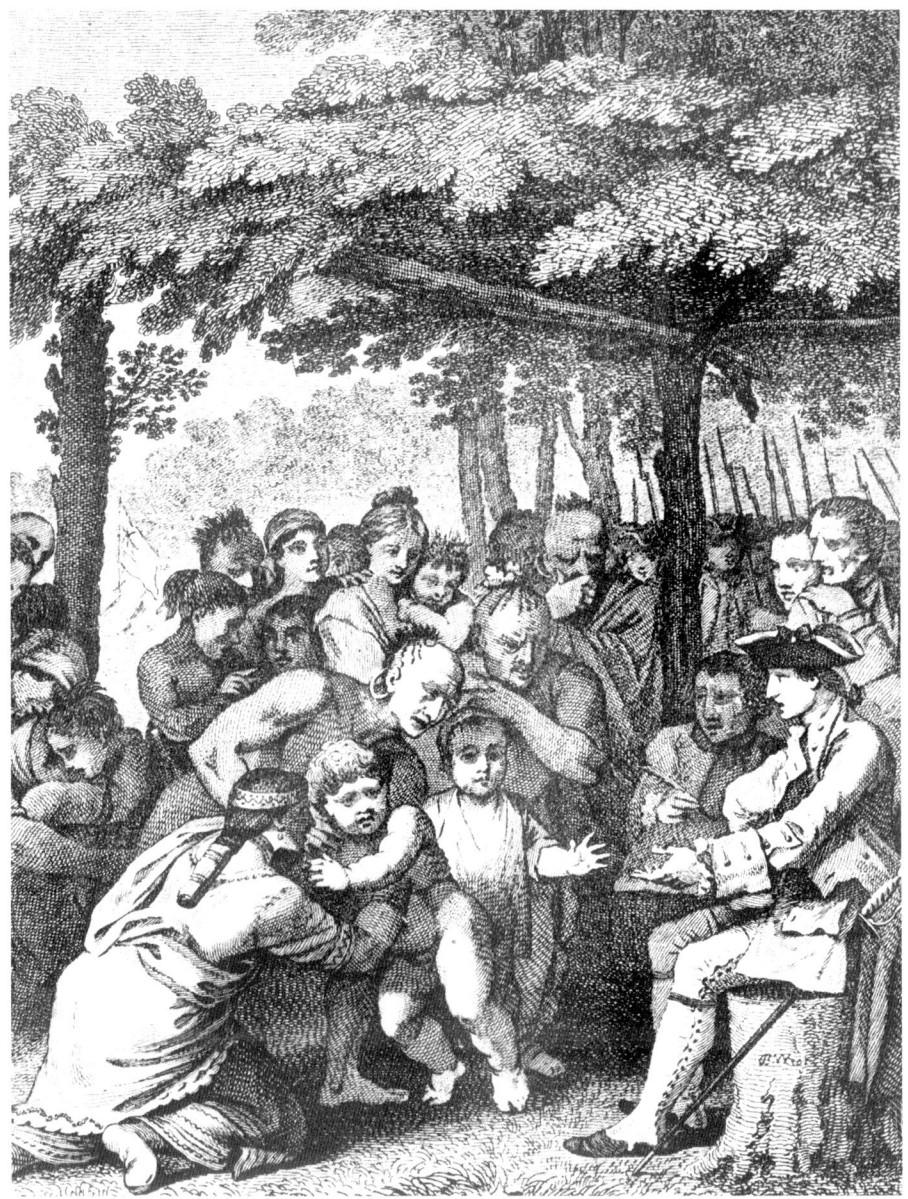

Illustration of Colonel Henry Bouquet retrieving English captives who had been assimilated into a tribe. *National Park Service, Fort Necessity National Battlefield.*

The First Frontier

the dim, misty forest and the expectation of an arranged ambush by native reenactors, gave these men what reenactors call a "period rush"—a feeling of being transported back in time to the event being recreated.

Most reenactors are a fascinating blend of exacting historian and little boy or girl playing dress-up, and it is that combination that makes them so engaging. These are "living historians" who love to talk to the public about what it is like to march miles in moccasins while wearing a wool uniform under a hot sun, or how to bake an apple pie in a Dutch oven using an open fire. But they also crave that period rush that often comes after the public leaves and darkness falls—when they can sit around the campfire under a starry sky, watch the sparks dance on the notes of a fiddle and suddenly—just for a moment—be transported to 1756.

First published in September 2005.

Our Elusive American Indian Story

Considering the impact that American Indians had on our region, it is not easy to learn their story. One quick glance at our place and river names prove that they were here: Aliquippa, Allegheny, Conemaugh, Juniata, Kiskiminetas, Kittanning, Loyalhanna, Mingo, Monongahela, Nemacolin, Ohiopyle and Youghiogheny—just to name a few—were derived from native names. But who coined those names originally? How long were they here? Where did they go?

We know that there were two basic tribal groups contending with each other, according to our region's earliest written histories: the Algonquins, whose most visible people in our region were the Leni-Lenape, or Delaware, and the Shawnee; and the Iroquois, represented here most commonly by the Seneca and Mingo. However, their relationships with one another—and even more so with Europeans—could be downright confusing. The Mingo, for example, lived here peaceably among Shawnee and Lenape. Depending on their assessment of the situation of the moment, Indian nations would side with the French at one point and then switch their allegiance if they sensed that the British were gaining the advantage. Sometimes the dynamics were personality based. The arrogance of British general Edward Braddock annoyed Indians to the point where they not only left the British camp but also fought for the French during the Battle of the Monongahela, at which Braddock was defeated and fatally wounded. Dedicated study is required just to understand the players and dynamics of that day.

Many of the people who sincerely want to educate us about Eastern Woodland Indians seem lacking in one way or another. Native American reenactors usually can be found at any eighteenth-century event. These "living historians" pride themselves on creating an accurate appearance but tend to be less knowledgeable about the culture and spirituality of their role models. You can also attend "powwows" sponsored by people who claim to be the contemporary embodiment of the Eastern Woodland Indians. Some can actually point to a bit of a bloodline. Most, though, are "adopted" and come off as New Age Indians.

Part of the problem is that our rugged terrain and harsh winters discouraged indigenous people from establishing permanent settlements in the region. These were summer hunting grounds for a variety of tribes. So the Lenape, Shawnee and others settled here in a few scattered villages for just a couple generations as they were being pushed westward by European settlers. Since no reservations were established within our region, the Eastern Woodland Indian culture that existed here is preserved only in oral traditions and scattered historical records of the period.

But what a period it is! These were the wild 1700s, and from those days we have stories of traders like John Hart and Peter Chartiers, the French and Indian War, Indian chiefs Captain Jacobs and Half-King and the Battle of Bushy Run; stories of Indians massacring settlers and settlers doing the same to Indians, of captures and escapes and of dark characters such as Louis Wetzel and Simon Girty, white men who lived among the Indians as "renegades." While the violent stories are fascinating, we know far less about how Indians lived, interacted with one another and thrived in this rugged place.

There is much to learn about our shared history with the Eastern Woodland Indians. Thankfully, with the ready availability of information on the Internet, the growth in the number and knowledge of native reenactors and the increased emphasis placed on native culture and spirituality by the powwow circuit, we all are growing in understanding—which is as it should be. For in discovering how these people lived here, we learn more about ourselves and this special place that they unwillingly left us.

First published in November 2003.

The First Frontier

History Can Teach Us about Us

The featured speaker was Dr. Matthew Ward from the University of Dundee, Scotland, who spoke on the social impact of the French and Indian War on the "back country" of Pennsylvania.

"It served to transform the peaceable kingdom of the seventeenth century into the Wild West of the eighteenth century," concluded Ward, speaking with a muted accent that blended his British nativity, years of higher education in the United States and current billet in Scotland. For an hour and a half, Ward had been moving between an overhead projector and the podium on the stage of the Ferguson Theater at the University of Pittsburgh at Greensburg, talking to an audience of about 150. While a fair number of students were there—including some, no doubt, who were told to come by their professors—a majority of the audience was older adults, compelled to be there only by their interest in this dynamic, colorful period of our history. This was an Arthur St. Clair Lecture, which is held each year to celebrate and explore Westmoreland County's contributions to our nation's history by bringing in distinguished scholars from across the county, or even across the pond.

What is really fascinating is what these historians from distant places can tell us about ourselves. Ward, for example, has found that Pennsylvania's frontier experience in the late 1600s and early 1700s differed distinctively from that of colonists in New England and the Carolinas. Because of the comparatively enlightened practices of the Penns—the proprietary government—and the fact that early Pennsylvania was populated mostly by pacifist Quakers and Germans, relations with the American Indians here were relatively peaceful during that period. Contrary to popular perception, most early Pennsylvania settlers and traders—just about all of whom lived east of here—didn't even use guns, according to Ward.

What the Europeans still refer to as the Seven Years' War—what we call the French and Indian War—changed everything. Indians turned hostile and terrorized colonial settlers. The settlers turned to guns and started responding to violence with violence. Traders put guns into the hands of the Indians—often with the tacit encouragement of the British or French authorities. Other factors were at work as well: more Europeans, particularly Scots-Irish who didn't feel welcome in the East, were migrating west and illegally squatting on land that belonged to Indian nations by treaty. Indians

Pennsylvania's Allegheny Mountains

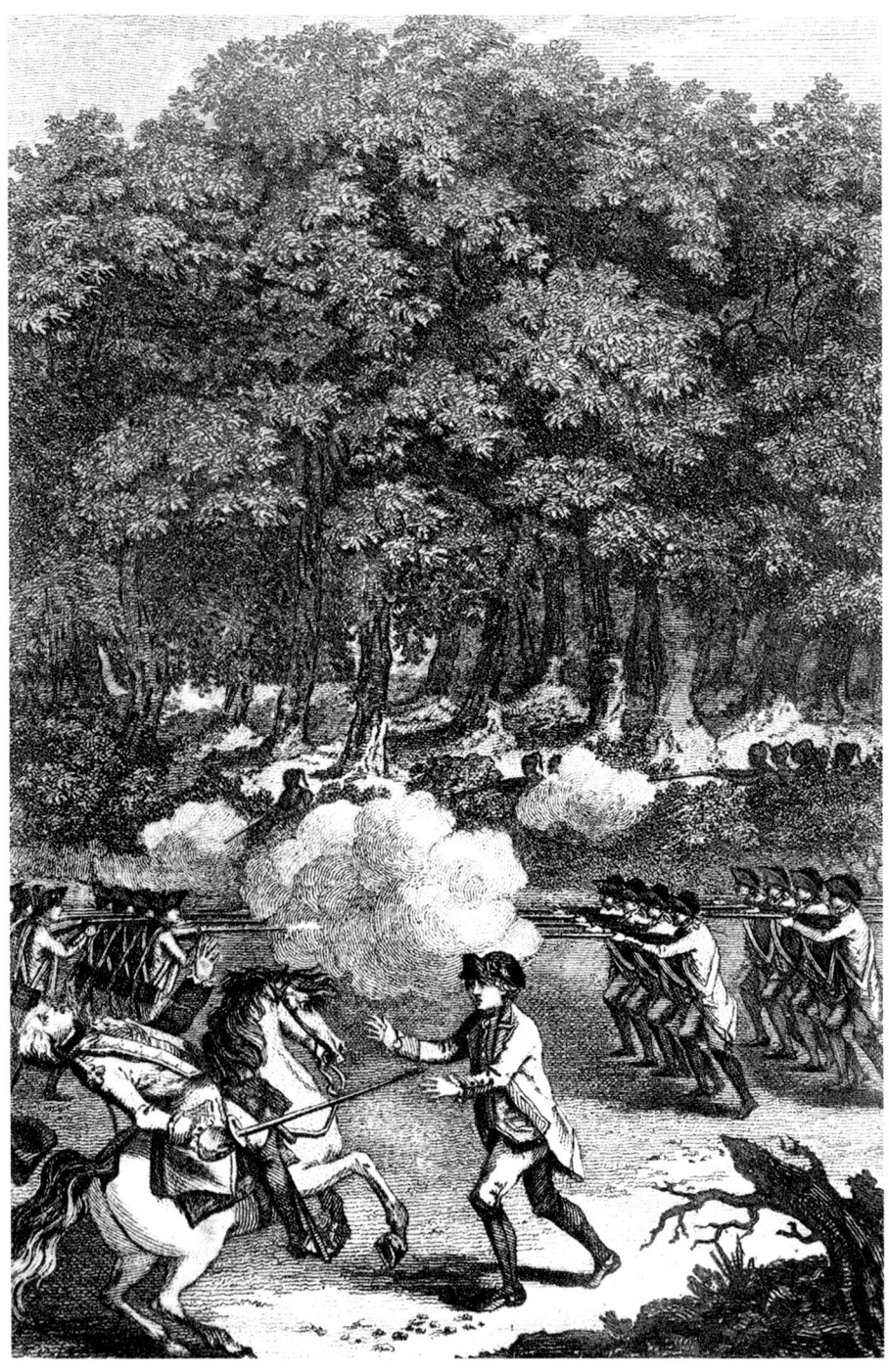

General Edward Braddock falls at the Battle of the Monongahela on July 5, 1755, with George Washington going to his assistance. *National Park Service, Fort Necessity National Battlefield.*

The First Frontier

became upset with the incursions and apparent treaty breaches. The Scots-Irish, who tended to be contentious by nature, were more than ready to protect their new homes. By the latter 1760s, once the Treaty of Fort Stanwix had opened our region to white settlement and drawn in many veterans of the war, a culture of guns and lawlessness gripped Pennsylvania's backcountry, truly turning it into the Wild West that has colored our perceptions of the period to this day, Ward said.

Ever wonder why the gun culture is strong here? Why so many of us are avid hunters? (Haven't you heard outsiders express surprise that the first day of deer season is a school holiday here?) The roots of that, Ward believes, extend to our region's experience during the French and Indian War, more than 250 years ago.

Whether you agree or disagree with Ward's perspective, isn't it remarkable that our region's histories attract such distinguished—and widespread—academic interest? Seize opportunities to experience lectures, seminars and other educational events focusing on the period of the French and Indian War. You may be surprised to learn what a historian from England knows about you.

First published in October 2004.

Let's Remember November 25

Pittsburghers just celebrated November 25 as their city's birthday, but we should remember this date, too—whether we consider ourselves Pittsburghers or not. November 25, 1758, was the day that British forces under the command of Brigadier General John Forbes claimed the strategically important Forks of the Ohio for the Crown. From the smoldering ruins of Fort Duquesne (which just had been abandoned and torched by the French) would rise Fort Pitt and, ultimately, Pittsburgh.

For Forbes, the end of his seven-month campaign had to feel somewhat anticlimactic. He had assembled a six-thousand-man expeditionary force of highlanders, Royal American regulars, provincial militia, Indian allies and artillery at Bedford and marched his army over the daunting Alleghenies. To protect supply lines, he had fortifications built along the way, including Fort Ligonier, which would serve as the staging area to attack Fort Duquesne. Forbes mediated a dispute between George Washington, who had wanted to use General Edward Braddock's military road (possibly due in part to personal business interests, many historians believe), and Colonel Henry Bouquet, who favored a new route from Bedford. Forbes decided in Bouquet's favor. Then there was the challenge of cutting a new military road wide enough for wagons through one hundred miles of wilderness over the Alleghenies. Upon reaching the outpost at Loyalhanna (afterward known as Fort Ligonier), Forbes's men suffered a serious defeat at the hands of French and Indian forces, who ambushed a British advance force outside the walls of Fort Duquesne in September, and then a near-disastrous friendly fire incident in early November that killed forty and later was described by Washington as the most dangerous moment in his military career. In between, on October 12, the British and provincials successfully repulsed an attack by French and Indian forces on Fort Ligonier. Then, acting on intelligence that the French forces in Fort Duquesne had lost their Indian allies and were in need of food and supplies, Forbes launched an assault to take the Forks before the onset of winter. On November 24, with Forbes's men still twelve miles from their objective, scouts returned with word that the fort at the Forks was burning.

Over the two and a half centuries since, so much has emerged from Fort Duquesne's ashes! This region became a gateway to the West. The Forks of the Ohio—we know them better as the Three Rivers—provided natural transportation resources that drew manufacturers here. Pittsburgh became known as a glassmaking center. Essentially, the nation's steel and aluminum industries were born and matured within the region. Connellsville coke set a world standard. Alcoa, Heinz, Mellon, U.S. Steel and Westinghouse became household names. The Smoky City started cleaning up and recreating itself in the mid-twentieth century. By the century's end, the now-smoke-free city had evolved into one of the nation's most livable communities, offering diverse employment opportunities, a colorful patchwork of urban and ethnic neighborhoods and a rich variety of recreational and cultural activities.

Now there's also much to celebrate in the way of achievements that took place during the period between 2003 and 2008, when our region observed its important place within the history of the French and Indian War. A $15 million four-hour dramatic documentary, *The War that Made America*, was produced and premiered on PBS stations nationwide. The documentary placed the often-overshadowed French and Indian War in its proper historical context—as the conflict that laid the groundwork for American independence. Permanent museum exhibits were developed at the Heinz History Center and Fort Ligonier. Significant artifacts from the period were

The First Frontier

The 1771 bill of sale by which George Washington purchased land that included the site of Fort Necessity. *National Park Service, Fort Necessity National Battlefield.*

secured: Fort Ligonier acquired George Washington's saddle pistols and his personal account of the period between 1753 and 1758 here. Fort Necessity National Battlefield received the original bill of sale dated 1771 through which Washington purchased the Great Meadows—the site of the fort and his only military defeat.

Our 250th commemorative activities may be over, but these resources will continue to attract visitors to our region. Our place in American history is now more prominent than it was. Our pride in our region should be deeper. All of this is because of the events that culminated on November 25, 1758.

So November 25 is a date worth remembering annually—as a time to recall our history and honor the people who, over the centuries since, have made this place special.

First published in November 2008.

Washington Wouldn't Approve of This

Perhaps your ancestors were among the thousands of settlers who were steadily trickling into this region by the 1790s. What a time to live here!

The Revolutionary War was over, but its passions still smoldered. While "Indian troubles" had ended, their memory was fresh in settlers' minds. This was still the frontier, the Ohio Country, and boundaries were uncertain. Pennsylvania claimed this region. So did Virginia. War veterans were showing up with conflicting land grants, issued by each commonwealth. Most residents here were subsistence farmers. Their one cash crop—rye distilled into whiskey—was carried east in kegs on horseback over rough mountain "roads" and sold for vital supplies of salt, tools, lead and gunpowder.

Overarching it all was a fledgling federal government, still determining what its roles and responsibilities should be and considering how to raise money to pay off its war debt. In 1791, U.S. Treasury secretary Alexander Hamilton threw the catalyst into this volatile, socio-political brew: a nine-cent-per-gallon excise tax on whiskey. The reaction here was violent. Veterans had just fought a war with the British in part over the issue of excise taxes. Settlers needed every penny they could make for life-sustaining supplies. What had distant governments—state or federal—done for them? Many here wanted to be independent, free of competing commonwealths, free even of the new United States. They wanted to establish a new territory called "Westsylvania."

On top of it all, this hated whiskey excise was levied on the still. That meant that every gallon of whiskey produced, whether for medicinal use at home or for sale, was taxed. That also meant that "inspectors of revenue" such as John Neville went onto private property to serve writs. When Neville rode onto the William Miller farmstead in southern Allegheny County to serve such a writ in 1794, he was chased off by gunfire. Two days later, a force of five hundred men went to Neville's home; two "Whiskey Boys" were killed and Neville's home was burned. The Whiskey Rebellion had begun.

The First Frontier

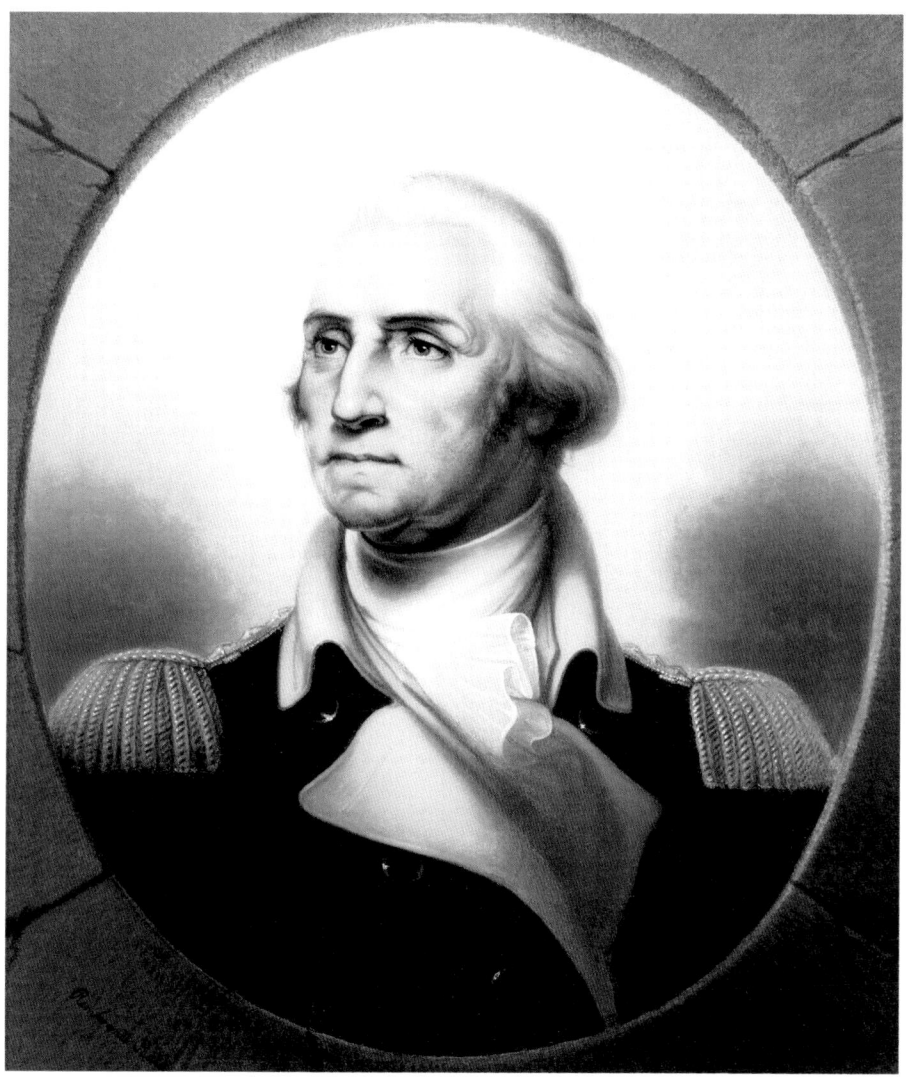

Porthole portrait of George Washington, circa 1824, by Rembrandt Peale (1778–1860), oil on canvas. *Westmoreland Museum of American Art, Greensburg, Pennsylvania. Gift of the William A. Coulter Fund.*

Responding to frontier-wide protests and harassment of tax collectors, President George Washington raised a federal army of thirteen thousand men and accompanied it as far as Bedford. Organized resistance disintegrated, and the force eventually arrested about twenty alleged insurrectionists who later were acquitted. The event—which earned a generous footnote in American history as the first test of the new federal government—echoes today in our attitudes of independence and self-reliance and suspicion of government; all of these are reasons to experience and remember this important piece of our heritage.

Friendship Hill was the Fayette County home of Albert Gallatin, a moderate political figure during the rebellion, who became U.S. Treasury secretary under President Thomas Jefferson. Now Gallatin's home near Point Marion is operated by the National Park Service. The home of William Miller's father, Oliver, still exists as a historical site in Allegheny County's South Park and hosts annual events that focus on the Whiskey Rebellion and eighteenth-century life. Neville's Woodville Plantation and Old St. Luke's Church—both in Allegheny County—and the David Bradford House in Washington, Pennsylvania, are other historical sites that interpret stories of the Whiskey Rebellion and hold special events relating to that period.

Experience this history for yourself—and don't be surprised to discover that there's a bit of Whiskey Boy (or Girl) in you, too.

First published in September 2004.

Johnny Appleseed Had Roots Here

Did you know that Johnny Appleseed's seeds came from our region? That means that orchards and apple trees across the upper Midwest actually have roots in the Allegheny Mountains of Pennsylvania.

Our heritage continually amazes me. Although I've been writing about it for twenty years, there's always something new to learn. Johnny Appleseed is my latest example. I'm not sure I even knew he truly existed, much less that he initially based his activities within western Pennsylvania. In 1774, Johnny was born John Chapman in Massachusetts. Such was the larger-than-life character of the man that there are as many myths and legends about him presented as facts. Various sources agree that he started his itinerant lifestyle early and was a nurseryman by the time he entered his twenties.

Johnny was also a Christian missionary who preached the teachings of a Swedish scientist and Lutheran reformist named Emanuel Swedenborg. What became known as the Church of New Jerusalem professed an intellectual theology that combined more scientific explanations of the Bible with a focus on the spiritual world, creating a material/spiritual connection that appealed to many people of the period. Among Swedenborg's earliest

The First Frontier

adherents in America was Maria Barclay's family in Philadelphia. In 1794, Maria married a Scottish lawyer named John Young, and shortly thereafter, they moved to land that Young had purchased in Greensburg, where he eventually became a judge. Somewhere in his early travels, John Chapman also became exposed to the writings of Swedenborg and embraced the New Jerusalem church. According to an article by Arthur F. Humphrey, published in *Westmoreland History* magazine, Chapman came to Greensburg, where he was nurtured in his faith by John and Maria Young.

Beginning about 1800, Chapman started to collect apple seeds from the pulp produced by cider presses in the Smithton, West Newton and Belle Vernon areas. Then he traveled up the Allegheny River Valley all the way into New York State, producing and distributing apple tree seedlings.

Here's where legend begins to do injustice to the man. Chapman wasn't just an eccentric wanderer, aimlessly scattering apple seeds. He would purchase a few acres of land, hack out and fence a clearing and establish a small nursery for seedlings. Then he would sell, trade or give the seedlings to settlers in that area. By the early 1800s, Chapman headed into the wilderness that would become Ohio and Indiana, acquiring bits of land, establishing nurseries and distributing seedlings. According to Humphrey, homesteaders were required to establish productive orchards within three years after their arrival. Johnny's seedlings simplified the meeting of such a requirement.

Chapman lived the simple lifestyle of an itinerant, constructing American Indian–type shelters, wearing ill-fitting clothing gained through bartering, often walking on heavily calloused bare feet and keeping only the simplest of possessions. European settlers and Indians alike respected him. Along with apple trees, he spread his faith and practiced it in his daily life. He became an authority on medicinal herbs, ate no meat and revered the lives of all creatures. But he also was an intuitive businessman who bought and sold dozens of tracts of land and then buried his money, using a system that enabled him to find his cash caches years later.

Each year until his death in 1845, according to Humphrey, Johnny Appleseed would return to Westmoreland County and to the pumice of cider mills there to gather his seeds. Perhaps he did this to see his fellow Swedenborgians, the Youngs. Perhaps the seeds grew well for him. Whatever the reason, if he did indeed return here regularly, then clearly he found something within our region that was worth sharing.

First published in September 2007.

Christmas by Candlelight

Luminaries light the way, serving as a warm glow in the cold night. Inside a home that has sheltered people from hundreds of winters, simple white candles burn in bunches of two and three at the center of a table, surrounded by crockery. A grandmotherly woman stands at the table, stirring ingredients in a large glazed bowl with a wooden spoon. Her face has a warm, ruddy glow in the flickering candlelight. Flames snap in a stone fireplace. Pine boughs, draped along the mantle, softly scent the room.

We can close our eyes and embrace these images with all of our senses. And at Christmastime, when we yearn for home and hearth, family and fellowship, such images touch us deeply. While twenty-first-century life blesses us with comforts undreamt of by our eighteenth-century ancestors, it bedevils us with complexities unknown to them. As we spend increasing amounts of time in stores, dealing with increasingly stressed customers and clerks, we don't tend to reflect on the days when a merry Christmas meant a hearty meal and one gift made by loving hands. As we untangle strings of lights with freezing fingers, we don't think about the beauty of a single candle's flame as it dances with the dark. Juggling schedules with distant family members for holiday gatherings, we don't consider the days when families lived under one roof or in the same hollow.

Nostalgia, of course, is rose-colored. Christmases here during the 1700s and early 1800s sometimes went uncelebrated. People tended to be preoccupied with survival. Holiday feasts took the form of whatever was at hand: some type of fowl, a dried-corn dish and maybe—for the fortunate ones—some fresh fruit from out east. Plum pudding, mincemeat pie and wassail—traditionally a nectar of ale, sugar and spices combined with the pulp of roasted apples—rounded out the repast. Gifts were few, unwrapped and given primarily to the children, usually some type of hand-carved wooden toy or game. There would have been no Christmas tree. That European tradition didn't find its way into homes here in America until the mid-nineteenth century. Santa Claus didn't exist then. (His birth came in 1823 with the publication of Clement Moore's "A Visit from St. Nicholas.") But bearded Belsnickel visited German households, bringing fruits, nuts and candy to good children and leaving lumps of coal or switches for the naughty ones. Christmas was celebrated, mostly, through the act of gathering with extended family and neighbors, usually at the church and generally for the day.

The First Frontier

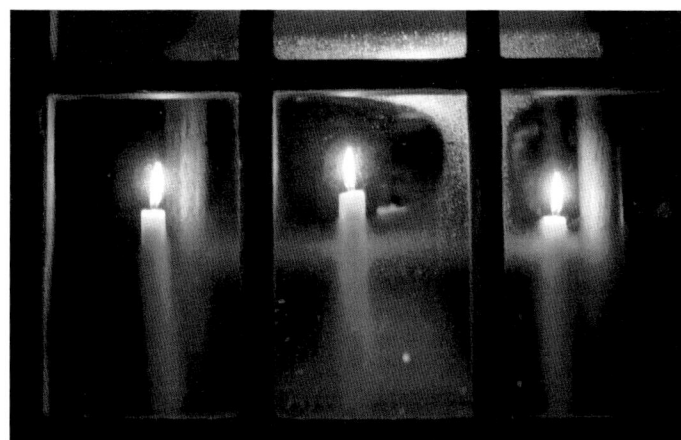

A candlelit holiday setting at Old Bedford Village, an eighteenth-century interpretive center in Bedford, Pennsylvania. *Photograph by Larry McKee.*

Perhaps it is that simplicity, that lack of clutter, that draws us. Perhaps the flame of a single candle symbolizes the hope of the Christ child better than a 100,000-light display. Perhaps the cracking fire speaks of home and family more eloquently than the best-written Christmas card.

Don't let the whirl of a twenty-first-century Christmas season spin your holiday spirit. There are two hundred years worth of perspective to be gained—and plenty of places to find it—when you experience eighteenth- and early nineteenth-century historical sites around the holidays. There's the Compass Inn Museum in Laughlintown on U.S. Route 30, a 1799 stagecoach stop; the David Bradford House in Washington, Pennsylvania, a Whiskey Rebellion site; Hanna's Town near Greensburg, a recreated frontier village; the LeMoyne House, also in Washington, which dates from the early 1800s; Old Bedford Village just outside Bedford, featuring eighteenth-century log homes; and the Woodville Plantation of John Neville in Bridgeville southwest of Pittsburgh, another Whiskey Rebellion site.

Take a little time from your hectic holiday schedule to experience Christmas by candlelight. Do it with your family or that special someone. You may receive a gift of Christmas spirit wrapped in heritage.

First published in November 2003.

PART IV

Working with the Alleghenies

Transportation Unlocked the Treasure

Life has never been simple amid Pennsylvania's Allegheny Mountains. Initial settlement was slow here, compared to other areas, because access was so arduous. That's why this region's transportation story is laced with such innovation. Once our nineteenth-century ancestors discovered ways to open these ridges to travel and commerce, however, the Alleghenies offered up a varied trove of resources. Fortunes were made. The population exploded. This region's products fueled the Industrial Revolution, settled the West, built great cities and provided much of the horsepower for a manufacturing engine that made America a world power.

The Alleghenies have been a demanding but generous partner, and the collaboration between man and mountains has produced the stuff of great stories. Just be ready to wipe off the sweat as you read them.

It's No Bull: Plastic Grows on Cows

When we think of the eighteenth century, our minds turn toward the glorious and the grim, to names like Washington and Braddock and Forbes, to musket barrages and scalpings and subsistence farming on the frontier, to epic stories worthy of the telling. However, there is equal marvel in the mundane, the details of how our eighteenth-century ancestors lived day to day. While some aspects sound very uncomfortable—powdered wigs and women's stays (used in corsets) come to mind—other particulars seem ingenious. Like this fact: they made combs from cow horns. Now I'm referring to good, fine-toothed combs; combs that I would run through my hair; combs that folded into protective, creatively shaped cases. How did they do that? Craftsmen known as "hornsmiths" did it, working with the horns of cows, bulls and oxen, which are composed of a mixture of keratin and gelatin (similar to our fingernails)—a kind of natural plastic.

"The cow horn is more versatile than any plastic we have today," Roland Cadle once told a group of twenty people during a program on hornsmithing at the Somerset Historical Center. Cadle, of Hollidaysburg, has spent the past thirty years researching and practicing traditional techniques of the craft.

Through the use of heat, pressure and moisture, horn could be turned on a lathe, flattened, split, welded and pressed into other forms. At three hundred degrees, horn loses the "memory" of its original form and adopts whatever shape is imposed on it, Cadle explained. Horn could be colored. It could be split and pressed into clear, transparent sheets. It could be etched with intricate designs. Spoons and dippers, containers, spectacles ("horn-rimmed glasses"), toys, drinking cups and, as mentioned, combs all could be made from horn. Combs actually were a mainstay for many hornsmiths, Cadle said. For comb-making, the horn had to be cut, heated and flattened while keeping the grain at an angle. Then it was pressed into a form and the teeth were cut against the grain for greater strength. Other articles—once common and now obsolete—were also made from horn, including lanthorns (from which lanterns evolved), scythe horns (holding accessories for scythes), inkhorns (portable ink and quill sets) and powder horns.

Today, powder horns are the best-known hornsmith product. Horn is an excellent container for black powder: nonmetallic yet waterproof and durable. The naturally shaped powder horns with which we are familiar were uniquely American, according to Cadle. European hornsmiths designed powder containers that didn't look like cow horns. But in eighteenth-century America, where almost everyone used guns, powder horns were in high demand, so hornsmiths kept them simple and produced as many as possible. Even small shops could turn out thousands of powder horns in a year. Still, hornsmiths found ways to distinguish their products from their competitors—primarily by varying the lathe pattern at the base and tip of the powder horn. Lathe patterns also changed with the styles of the times—often following furniture-lathing patterns—so today they provide clues to the age of antique powder horns.

The First Frontier

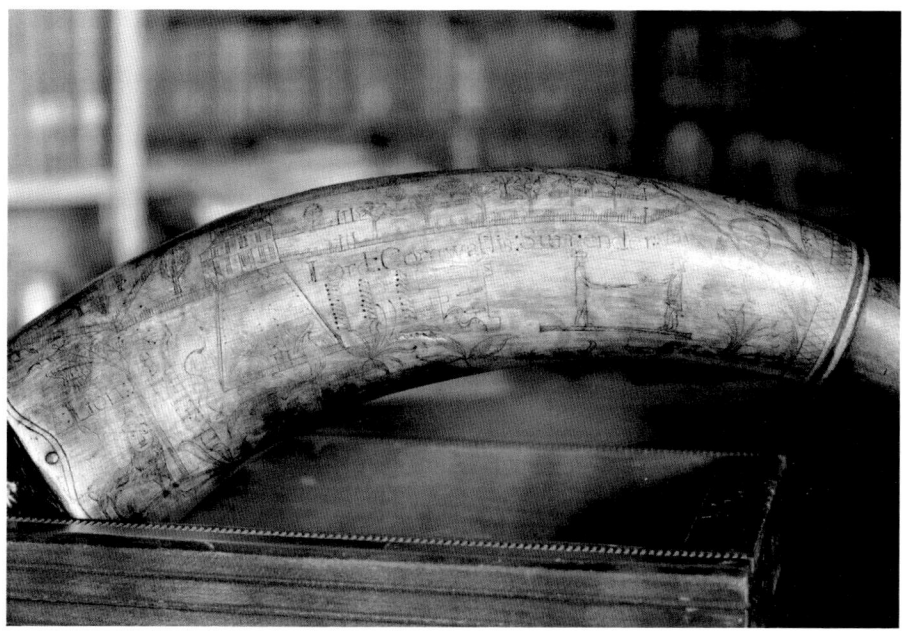

An example of an engraved powderhorn dating to the eighteenth century. *Historic American Buildings Survey, Library of Congress.*

Other pioneer crafts are the equal of hornsmithing in the amazement category: coopers, for example, created barrels, buckets, tubs and other liquid containers from wood. You've probably seen blacksmiths demonstrating how to work with iron, but did you know that there also were whitesmiths who worked with tin and pewter? Stonemasons' work can still be seen today around our region in bridge abutments, culverts, canal lock walls and even tunnel portals that have remained intact for more than 150 years—without the use of mortar. Weavers, carpenters, wheelwrights, furniture makers, tatters (lace-makers) and scrimshanders (engravers) all produced incredible products from the simplest of materials: wood, stone, horn, iron, fabric, glass and paper, among others.

Keep your eyes open for museum and historical site exhibits of eighteenth- and early nineteenth-century crafts. There are annual festivals that also feature them. Go. Be amazed by the mundane.

First published in September 2005.

PENNSYLVANIA'S ALLEGHENY MOUNTAINS

Our Window on the Past Is Open

Heavy mists lifted skyward from the far hillside as a light rain fell steadily. I looked past the water droplets dangling from the brim of my ball cap, to imagine the scene 248 years earlier:

The rain-soaked stockade brooded over the wagon teams lined up on the rough-cut roadway just below. Slowly, teamsters brought their loaded wagons down the bank toward the ford at Juniata Crossings, gripping halters, alternately cursing and encouraging horses and mules amid the tortured screech of locked, iron-banded wagon-wheels sliding across bedrock.

There are special places around our region where you can literally reach back 250 years and touch a time—so different from our own—when this was an almost trackless wilderness that taxed traveler and beast. My guide, Mike Burk, and I were in such a place: Juniata Crossings, six miles east of Everett and a half-mile north of its Pennsylvania State Historical Marker along U.S. Route 30. The familiar blue-and-gold cast-metal sign tells of the place where British general John Forbes's military road crossed the Raystown Branch of the Juniata River in 1758. Fortifications were erected there to protect the ford and enable Forbes's force to maintain communications. Letters penned by Forbes, George Washington, Henry Bouquet (Forbes's second-in-command) and others make references to the Crossings. A map of the fortifications there still exists among Bouquet's preserved papers.

Mike and I knew that we were in the right spot because we were looking at pronounced grooves—each easily three inches deep, three to four inches wide and at least three feet long—lined up in two pieces of bedrock on the hillside leading down to the ford. Iron rims of wagon wheels had worn these grooves over the 60 years that the Crossings were used. They offer silent testimony to the challenges endured by those who simply desired to travel here. Just below the grooves on the valley floor is an impressive structure of dry-laid shaped stone, fifty feet wide, twenty feet high and eight feet thick. This was a supporting abutment for a chain suspension bridge that spanned the Juniata here at some point prior to 1818, when a two-lane covered bridge was built upstream to replace the Crossings. Local lore has Bouquet's men building the suspension bridge, but the craftsmanship displayed in the abutment (which remains impressively intact despite 250 years of frequent flooding), and reports that the suspension chain was made of hand-forged iron links eight

The First Frontier

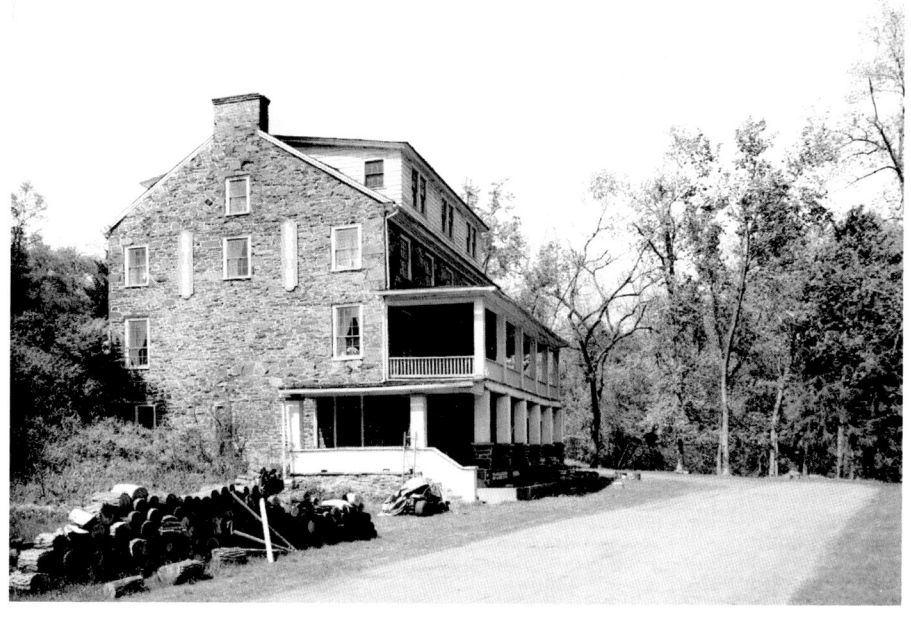

Dennison Tavern, built in 1818 along the former Chambersburg-Bedford Turnpike near Juniata Crossings. *Photograph by Jet Lowe, Historic American Buildings Survey, Library of Congress.*

inches long and four inches across, suggest a more involved public works project—perhaps during improvements to Forbes Road circa 1790.

With the snows of winter gone but spring's growth just beginning, we could easily trace the wagon trail above the rock grooves. Standing below them at the water's edge, Mike could illustrate the "debris fan" of sediment and rock that—over time—had washed down the hillside into the Raystown Branch at this spot, making it a favorable ford.

History is written across our region's rugged landscape, waiting to be read during this period that local National Park Service historians refer to as "leaf-off." It's an annual window into our past that's open only for a few short weeks. Now's the time to explore your favorite historical site and see what usually lies hidden under greenery, fallen leaves and snow. Or experience a new place (please respect property rights) and then do some research to learn more about what you've seen.

This may not be the prettiest time of year, and the weather can be uncomfortable, but freed from the distractions of lush scenery, our senses can focus on the details that make our history come alive.

First published in April 2006.

Waterways Are Heritage Highways

Traveling U.S. Route 22 southwest of Altoona and approaching that jumble of imposing hills known as the Allegheny Front usually prompts a sense of appreciative awe. What we casually, comfortably cross on a fine, multilane highway in minutes once required days of arduous trekking on foot or many hours on the Allegheny Portage Railroad. We tend to forget the day when rivers were the only highways through this region.

Back in colonial times, this was known simply as the "wilderness," an intimidating maze of mountains and trackless old-growth forests inhabited by scattered communities of native people. Even before the arrival of Europeans, Iroquois and Algonquin tribes competed for control of the region's waterways because it also meant control of commerce, which in those days was fur trade. As European traders such as John Hart started wandering here, they followed the old native paths that, whenever possible, followed the waterways. Lead mining took place in Sinking Valley just east of the Front as early as the 1760s, and much of the smelted lead was shipped on the adjacent Little Juniata River. In 1771, the Pennsylvania General Assembly declared the Juniata River to be a public stream and highway. By the early 1800s, "Juniata Iron" was being produced in ironworks along the Little Juniata and the Juniata's Frankstown Branch. That early pig iron and processed iron was also carried by wagon to Johnstown, where it was loaded onto flatboats and shipped down the Conemaugh, Kiskiminetas and Allegheny Rivers to Pittsburgh for use by blacksmiths to make iron implements, horseshoes and wheel rims.

The Pennsylvania Main Line Canal turned the Allegheny Mountains' rivers into busy shipping corridors. In just the first year of 1834, 1,100 boats passed Huntingdon. From July 1 through July 20 in 1835, 680,000 pounds of freight were logged. By the next year that figure had jumped to 2.7 million pounds for the same time period. During the canal's most active period, boats were passing in twenty-minute intervals and only two to three of those daily were dedicated passenger boats. The remainder were either freight or freight-passenger vessels. Larger boats ran both day and night and carried crews of up to eight or nine. Shipping costs from Philadelphia to Pittsburgh, which had been as high as $120 to $220 per ton in 1800, dropped dramatically to $20 per ton by 1835.

Because the Pennsylvania Railroad ran its mainline through these same river valleys, the rivers remained part of the Alleghenies' transportation

The First Frontier

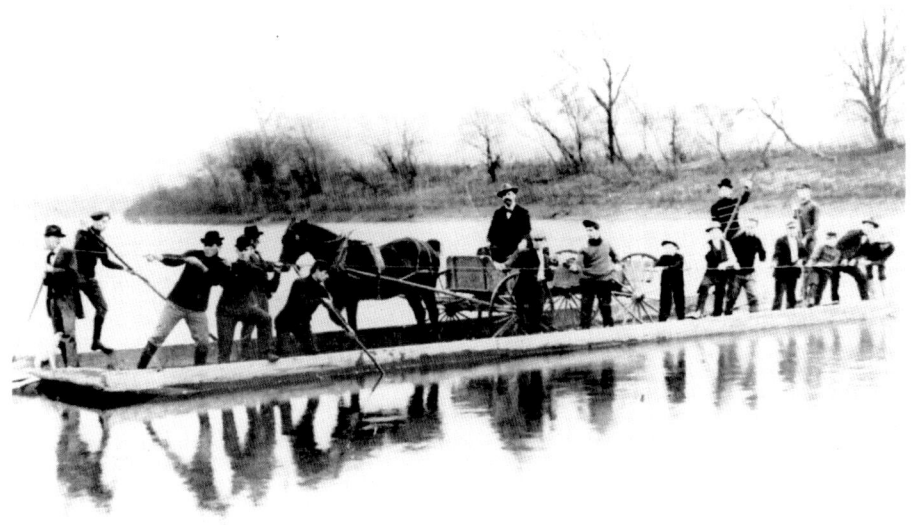

A rope ferry carries a horse-drawn wagon across the Juniata River. *Huntingdon County Historical Society Collection.*

corridors long after they stopped carrying much traffic themselves. Mills, plants and communities became established along their banks. Their water was tapped for both human and industrial consumption. Unfortunately, they also received much of our waste. For most of the twentieth century, our rivers struggled to sustain life, and the communities along the banks turned their backs. However, a drastic reduction in industrial and mining activity, stricter environmental regulations and effective treatment of discharges have enabled our rivers to rebound over the past quarter-century. They are growing healthier and being rediscovered.

So much of our history and heritage is carried by our humble little mountain rivers with names such as Casselman, Conemaugh, Juniata, Kiskiminetas, Stonycreek, Youghiogheny and West Branch (Susquehanna)! And some of our region's most beautiful places can be seen best from their points of view. The Little Juniata's golden-chocolate waters have carried me through the mint-green corridor that is tree-lined Barree Canyon. Upon weathering one of the Youghiogheny's rapids, I've seen the exuberant rush of a tributary's hillside cascade. And I've shared a Main Line Canal traveler's view approaching the canal port of Leechburg as it emerges on a bend in the Kiskiminetas. You can have such experiences, too. Just climb out of your vehicle and step into a canoe or kayak.

May and June are especially good times to do so because annual river sojourns are scheduled on most of the Pennsylvania Alleghenies' rivers. Sojourners don't just paddle a river, they learn about it through scheduled programs that explore the featured river's history, natural features, ecology and environmental challenges.

Our highways may offer convenience, comfort and expediency while traveling across our rugged landscape. But waterways still provide our best passages through Pennsylvania's Alleghenies.

Early Spring Is Canal-Trace Season

My guide, Mike Burk of Ebensburg, and I were feeling fortunate. Instead of the cold, continuous rain predicted, we had been hiking in relatively dry and comfortable conditions for more than an hour. Bushwhacking along a bank of the Conemaugh River within the Packsaddle Gap, a couple of miles upstream from Blairsville, we were picking careful paths along steep, wooded slopes and through rock fields. The predicted rain would have made this terrain treacherous.

Our objective sat amid a thicket of browned and brittle Japanese knotweed stalks: an amazingly intact Lock 5 of the Pennsylvania Main Line Canal, with its two parallel walls of 175-year-old cut-stone in better condition than most residential retaining walls. Ten feet of water separated its sides. One had an indentation about five feet long with the stones at the near end cut concavely; half of an iron lock gate had been anchored here and nested within the indentation to permit passage of the boat. Another concave cut in the opposite wall had held the hinge for the gate's other half. I marveled at the handwork that went into this lock. Four courses of stonework were visible above the waterline, and these locks were at least fifteen feet deep. Brawny Irish immigrants formed the massive blocks from native stone with black powder, hammers and chisels. One block I measured was seven and one-half feet long, twenty-two inches across and thirteen inches high—and its faces were almost as true as those of a molded brick.

"Marvel" is an apt reaction to the Pennsylvania Main Line Canal story, given the monumental size of the enterprise and the extent to which it affected our region. The Juniata Division ran for 127 miles from the Susquehanna River to Hollidaysburg, featured 88 locks, 25 covered aqueducts, more than 100 bridges, 17 dams and hundreds of culverts and

The First Frontier

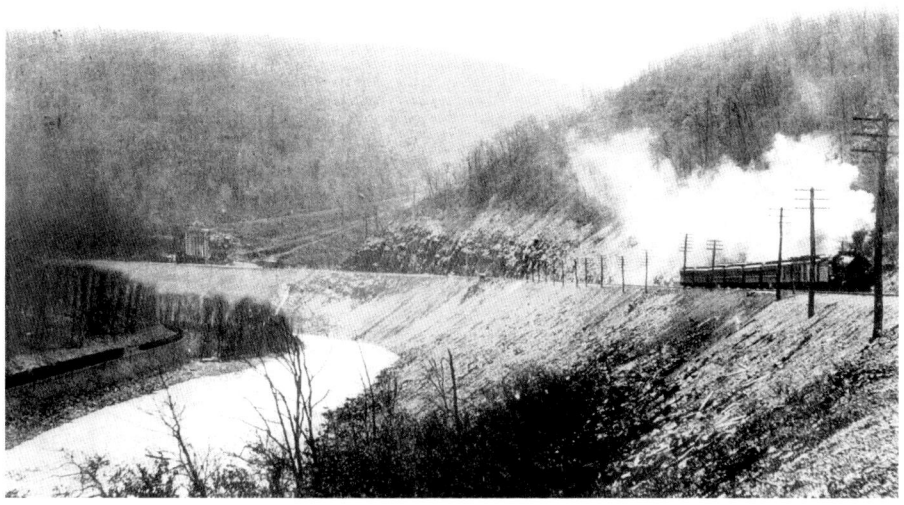

An undated postcard of a steam train emerging from the Packsaddle Gap along the Conemaugh River. *Blairsville Improvement Group and the Historical Society of the Blairsville Area.*

waste-weirs. The Western Division from Johnstown to Pittsburgh was 103 miles in length with 60 locks, 16 covered aqueducts, 152 bridges, 10 dams, 64 culverts, 39 waste-weirs and 2 of the first tunnels in the United States. Connecting the two divisions and carrying canalboats over the mighty Allegheny Front, the Allegheny Portage Railroad was an engineering wonder of the early nineteenth century. Using the system of ten inclines, featuring steam-powered stationary engines, the Portage Railroad hauled passengers and freight up 1,400 feet to the top of the front, then transported them for 36 miles between Hollidaysburg and Johnstown.

The Pennsylvania Main Line Canal story should be experienced, and now is the time—before the groundcover grows and hardwoods sprout their leaves. While the Packsaddle Gap is inaccessible for many, other interesting canal traces can be seen easily. Within the Juniata Division east of Altoona, Lock 61 is well-preserved and located right along the Lower Trail. Gentle footpaths and trails within the Allegheny Portage Railroad National Historic Site near Cresson offer easy access to outstanding examples of culverts and retaining walls. Within the Western Division, you can see traces of the canal prism (channel) and towpath at the Tunnelview Historic Site just below the Conemaugh River Dam near New Alexandria. Or you can walk the West

Penn Trail upriver from Saltsburg and see portions of the canal prism and towpath, cut-stone walls and a lock depression in the area of White Station, about two miles from Saltsburg.

Just don't wait for an ideal weather forecast. Before you know it, these traces will be covered again for another growing season. Besides, as Mike and I found, meteorologists can always be mistaken.

First published in April 2005.

A Historic Landmark that Still Works

You don't have to be a rail fan to be impressed with the Horseshoe Curve. Just consider for a moment what it is, what it has meant and what it's doing now. This national historic landmark, which enables trains to clear the massive hurdle of the Allegheny Front, is as functional today as it first was in 1854. If there is an elegance to engineering, then the Pennsylvania Railroad created a civil work of beauty. Trains entered the Curve at an elevation of 1,594 feet and, in the process of rounding a 220-degree arc, climbed a critical 120 feet along a grade on which mid-nineteenth-century locomotives were capable of hauling freight. Upon leaving the Curve, the trains had gained enough elevation to continue their climb in straightforward fashion to the Allegheny Tunnel and the summit.

Ingeniously executed by engineers and surveyors, who plotted a track layout that has remained basically unchanged for 150 years, it was heroically and laboriously carved with picks, shovels, black powder and mules by hundreds of mostly Irish laborers. Once the Horseshoe Curve opened in 1854, the Port of Philadelphia competed successfully with ports in New York City and Baltimore. Our region's coal, lumber, steel and related products had markets both east and west. The Horseshoe Curve lifted us into the industrial age, exchanged raw materials for finished goods and transported labor, culture and new life here.

One measure of its importance is the attention that it has drawn in times of war. During the early summer of 1863, Confederate general Robert E. Lee brought his Army of Northern Virginia into Pennsylvania with the thought of marching on Altoona to capture the extensive railroad works there and the Horseshoe Curve. The tactical disadvantage posed by the terrain between Lee and Altoona, and the news that the Union Army of the Potomac was

The First Frontier

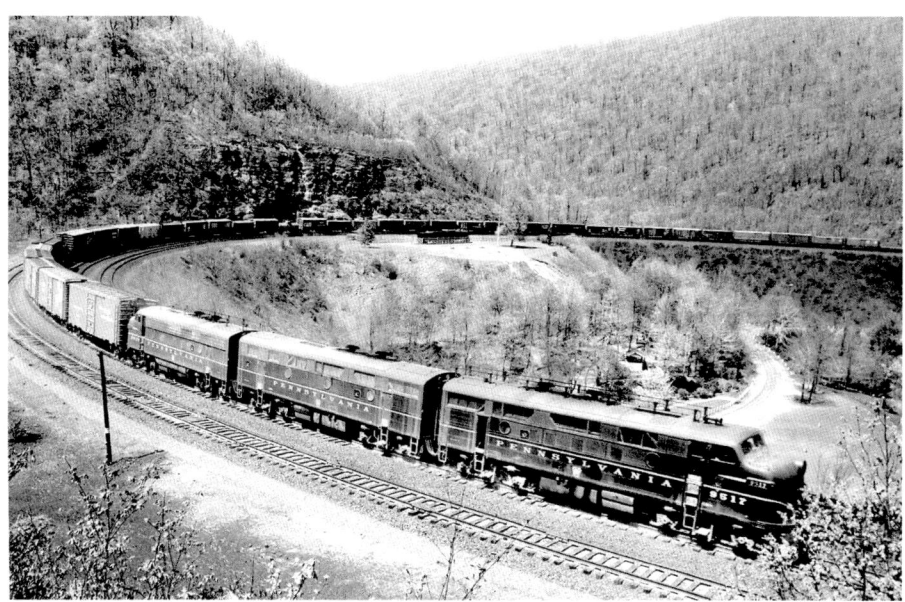

A Pennsylvania Railroad freight train rounds the Horseshoe Curve in the 1950s. *David Seidel Collection.*

marching northward, diverted Lee to Gettysburg instead. During both world wars, the Horseshoe Curve was guarded to prevent sabotage.

Over the century and a half since 1854, this region has seen its manufacturing base largely disappear. Road systems and airlines have replaced railroads as people movers and, these days, more people are leaving the region than migrating to it. Yet the Horseshoe Curve remains a vital part of the nation's shipping system, and rail fans have come to regard it as a railroad mecca.

Generations of photographers have captured the enduring image of a long freight train tracing the entire arc at one time, with its locomotive leaving the Horseshoe Curve as the caboose enters. One of the most famous pictures was snapped for the Curve's 100th birthday on October 20, 1954, by the Sylvania Electric Products Company to promote its "Blue Dot" flashbulbs. The photo was taken at night, illuminated by 6,500 flashbulbs, and published in *Life* magazine and newspapers across the country. For the Curve's 150th birthday, Sylvania came back and did it again—this time with train-mounted searchlights, one hundred strobe lights, halogen lights inside the railcars of a 2,500-foot-long train and section-by-section track lighting. While the 1954 lightshow was over in a fraction of a second, the 2004 show was continuous and climaxed with a fireworks display.

Now both a national historic landmark and a national engineering landmark, the Curve has a visitors' center, a park and train-viewing areas. It carries special trains, hauled by classic locomotives, during an annual Railfest. Amid the accolades, attention and honors, the Horseshoe Curve continues to do what it has done so faithfully since 1854: lift heavy burdens, overcome obstacles and bring life to the region.

First published in June 2004.

All the World Loved Connellsville Coke

In his conservative gray suit and red-and-white striped tie, and with his refined English accent and fringe of clipped white hair, Dr. Kenneth Warren did nothing to dispel the stereotype of the typical Oxford University professor. He was speaking to a mixture of 150 adults and students in the University of Pittsburgh at Greensburg's Ferguson Theater about a subject on which he is considered to be a leading scholar: the coke industry of Connellsville.

Simply put, the coal fields of Westmoreland, Fayette, Washington and Allegheny Counties were among the most productive in the nation from 1880 through 1920, and the coke developed from the coal of the Connellsville area set the world standard for quality. Connellsville coke contributed to the establishment of Pittsburgh as a steelmaking center, it made a fortune for Henry Clay Frick and it drew thousands of European immigrants here to mine coal and operate beehive coke ovens.

In the personification of H.C. Frick, Connellsville coke also captured the attention of a young doctoral student named Warren freshly graduated from the University of Cambridge, who was spending a year at the University of Wisconsin looking for comparisons between the British and American steel industries. For fifty years since, Dr. Warren has returned to the subject again and again, writing books about Frick, the Connellsville coke industry and—most recently—the United States Steel Corporation. Asked what it was about our region's history that has held an English scholar's interest all of these years, Dr. Warren responded that first, it was Frick, and then, the story of Connellsville coke.

By the 1860s, the coal of the Pittsburgh seam—especially the Connellsville sector—was found to produce high-quality coke (through a baking process that removed coal's more volatile components, enabling it

The First Frontier

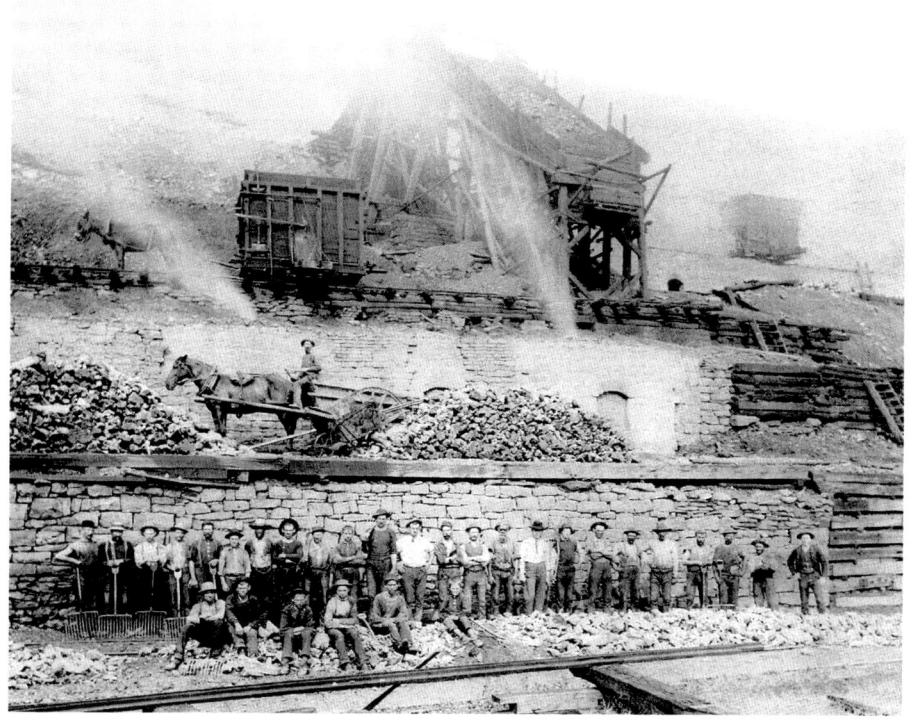

Workers at a bank of early coke ovens with mule-drawn lorries circa 1890. *Coal and Coke Heritage Center, Pennsylvania State University–Fayette, Eberly Campus, Ludwig Collection.*

to burn hotter, thus providing an excellent fuel for steelmaking). Soon the first beehive coke ovens started to appear. Anywhere from five to ten feet high and ten to thirteen feet across, these brick structures could turn about seven tons of coal into coke in forty-eight hours. With some of the world's best coke in its backyard, readily available by rail, Pittsburgh mushroomed as a steelmaking center.

From 1870 through 1910, Pennsylvania produced most of the nation's coke—and most of Pennsylvania's coke came from the Connellsville region. By the time Connellsville coke production peaked in the first decade of the 1900s, there were forty-three thousand beehive ovens here, according to Dr. Evelyn Hovanec of the Coal and Coke Heritage Center in Uniontown. But the development of by-product coke ovens (which produced other products in addition to coke) at integrated steel plants and the gradual depletion of coal in the Connellsville sector sent its coke industry into decline. By the 1930s, 90 percent of the nation's coke was being produced in by-product ovens.

As Dr. Warren reflected on the dramatic rise and fall of Connellsville coke, he displayed images on a stage screen. One showed two long parallel lines of crumbling beehive ovens at Allison near Brownsville. "It just seems to me unbelievable that one should have such spectacular artifacts just wasting away," Dr. Warren told his audience, suggesting that some of these coal and coke sites should be preserved and presented to the public. "In my country, all the beehive coke ovens have disappeared. But you still have them here."

If all of these ovens disappear, we will have lost important physical links to this great American story and monuments to the hard work, the hazards and the accomplishments of our ancestors. While we don't need an Oxford education to grasp the seriousness of such a loss, the fact that an Oxford scholar is telling us suggests that we should listen.

First published in October 2003.

Celebrate Coal Mining

The coal miner is not extinct in our region, but this sometimes-ornery, often-colorful critter deserves endangered-species status—and our respect.

What made a bigger mark on our region than coal mining? Coal mined here—first by hand, then by machine—heated homes and businesses, fed steamship and locomotive engines, fired blast furnaces and turned power turbines. In the late nineteenth and early twentieth centuries, our region led Pennsylvania which in turn led the nation in the production of coal. The coal industry changed our landscape. Hundreds of mines and thousands of coke ovens were developed and later abandoned. Waste piles pimpled the landscape and many remain. Unnaturally colored streams still carry mine-leached metals.

The coal industry changed our cultural landscape as well, drawing emigrant workers and their families from central and southern Europe and African Americans from the South to little coal patches that still dot the map. Families crammed into inadequate company housing, cultivated backyard gardens and made American dreams come true through a work ethic that is almost unimaginable today. During the hand-loading era, which lasted well into the 1930s, miners were paid by the ton for back-bending, daily twelve-hour shifts in mines that were poorly regulated for safety. Families struggled with marginal income and company control of their lives. Women raised

The First Frontier

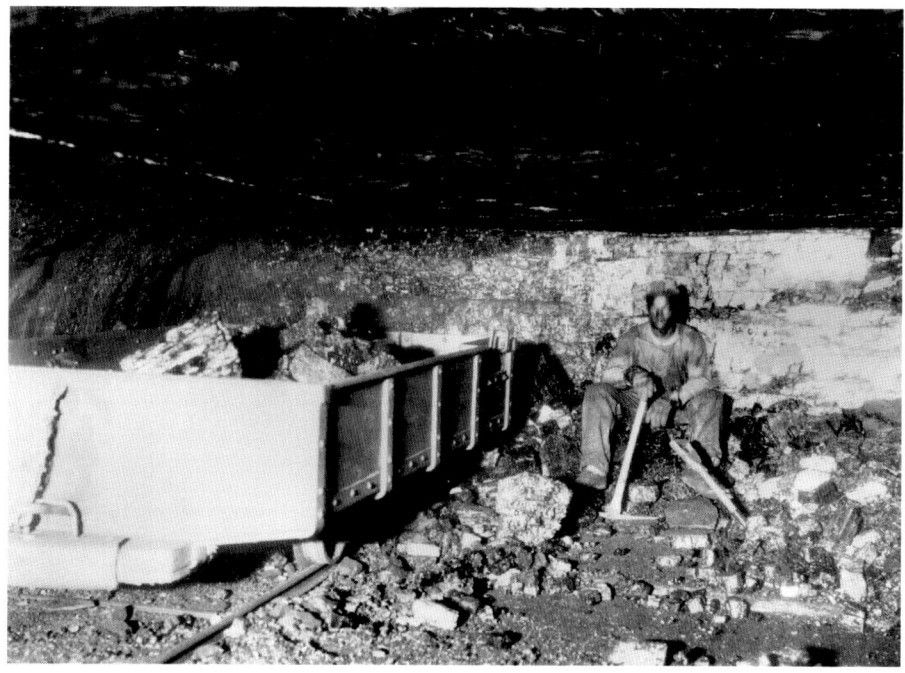

A miner sits at the face of the Yukon Mine of the Imperial Coal Company during the hand-loading era. *Johnstown Area Heritage Association.*

children and gardens, constantly scrubbed coal dust from their men and their home and froze in fear every time the siren announced an accident. Underground hazards and a common adversary—"the Company"—united miners and their families. Union and community blended to form a culture unique to the coal fields.

Mechanization, World War II and unionization turned our coal fields into a new world with good incomes for miners and profits for coal operators—for a couple of decades. But mining employment started to decline as early as the 1950s and dropped precipitously in the early 1980s. Today, there are just a few thousand miners employed in scattered operations around the region. Daily obituaries report the passing of another old roof-bolter or motorman.

Our region's coal heritage is too precious to lose. Fortunately, efforts are being made to preserve it in small mining museums, historical sites and even mining festivals.

Seldom Seen Tourist Coal Mine near Patton in northern Cambria County takes visitors underground for a taste of a genuine coal mine. Mining museums within the region include the Broad Top Area Coal Miners Museum in

Robertsdale, southern Huntingdon County and the Windber Coal Heritage Center. There's also a historical site commemorating the Quecreek miners' dramatic "9 for 9" rescue near Somerset.

The northern Somerset County community of Windber was built by the Berwind-White Coal Company to be the regional headquarters for its thirteen-mine operation there. Four million tons of "Eureka smokeless coal" were produced by Windber-area mines in 1910 alone, powering New York City's subway system and transoceanic steamships. Today the community celebrates its heritage with an annual Miners' Memorial Day weekend.

Greene County, which sits in the southwest corner of the state, is one of the last remaining pockets of active coal mining in Pennsylvania. For more than fifty years, the Greene County community of Carmichaels has been celebrating the industry with the Pennsylvania Bituminous Coal Show.

Participate in one of these coal-mining events or visit one of these sites and you'll experience one of our region's most distinctive ways of life—and have an enjoyable time doing it.

First published in June 2004.

The Year's First Sweet Reason to Travel

A web of blue, five-sixteenth-inch plastic lines zigzag from maple tree to maple tree as though spun by a crazy spider hopped up on PVC. At each tree, the blue "lateral" receives a black "drop" line from a black plastic spile—a two-and-one-half-inch tube that draws sap from the maple. The laterals gradually run downhill and eventually connect to one-inch black "mains" that carry the sap for hundreds of yards and then deposit it into collection tanks. It's maple season in the sugarbush, when producers endure the often-bitter conditions of winter-meeting-spring to produce sweet maple syrup and maple sugar products.

"You look forward to it every spring—tapping and the first smell of the syrup," Ed Emerick told me as we stood in the sugarbush that he and his son work near Wellersburg in southeastern Somerset County.

Just as a spile taps the sap of the sugar maple, so maple production taps our region's heritage. The earliest European settlers observed American Indians making sloping gashes into the sapwood of sugar maples. A knife or wood chip stuck into the bottom of the gash directed the sugar water

The First Frontier

into hollowed logs or water-tight bark baskets on the ground. Once enough of the sap had been collected into a hollowed log, fire-heated stones were placed inside to boil off the water. Settlers quickly improved the efficiency of the process. By the Revolutionary War, they were boring holes and using wooden spiles; by the nineteenth century, they were using buckets, called "keelers"; and by the 1870s, the keelers were being covered. Plastic tubing and collection lines started replacing buckets in the 1960s. Originally, settlers boiled off the sap in kettles over fires. By the 1840s, "sugar houses" or camps were putting the process under roof, and large evaporator pans were being used. Generations of Somerset County farming families have been refining the process ever since.

Today, sap is collected through the plastic lines and ends up at a sugar camp like that of Christine and Everett Sechler. Christine calls herself the "Mistress of the Filtering Process," which is the final step of maple syrup production. When the syrup emerges from the evaporator, she measures it for proper density (basically, a weight of eleven pounds per gallon), adds

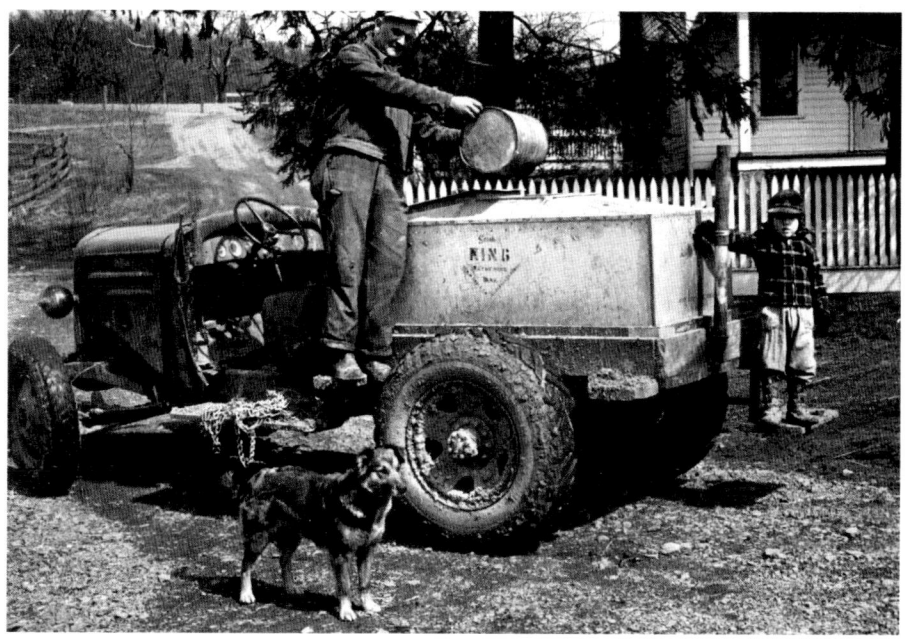

Earle Sechler pours sap into a collection tank in 1955–56 with his son, Everett, then age five. *Christine and Everett Sechler.*

"diatomaceous earth" (basically, crushed seashells) to bond with remaining impurities and then filters out the resulting paste before storing the syrup in thirty-eight-gallon stainless-steel drums. Everett showed me the earlier stages of the process: collected sap is run through a reverse-osmosis machine to draw off 70 percent of the water; the more concentrated (8 percent) sugar water is exposed to ultraviolet light to kill bacteria and then enters the stainless-steel evaporator. Fresh sugar water enters the back section of the evaporator and travels through three long and narrow channels, becoming progressively heavier as it boils. Moving into the front section, it churns its way through another three channels. When the syrup reaches a specific temperature (set this day between 214.4 and 214.6 degrees Fahrenheit) in the final channel, an automatic draw-off thermometer determines that the syrup has reached the proper density and drains it into a stainless-steel bucket. The bucket is carried to Christine's filtering station.

Opportunities to experience maple production provide the year's first good reason for travel (for those who are not winter-sports enthusiasts). And for those who travel on their stomachs, this is the best time to enjoy Pennsylvania pork sausage and pancakes, smothered with fresh maple syrup. The Shaver's Creek Environmental Center holds an annual Maple Harvest Festival. Then there's the granddaddy, the Pennsylvania Maple Festival, which dates to the day back in 1947 when Kate Smith, the legendary entertainer, pronounced Somerset maple syrup to be the best she'd ever tasted on her national radio program.

When you sample our region's maple products, you are sharing a taste enjoyed by Eastern Woodland Indians, eighteenth-century settlers and Kate Smith—as well as by generations of Emericks and Sechlers. So throw off the lap robe and brave the unpredictable weather. Oh and don't worry, there really aren't any PVC-crazed spiders in the sugar bush.

First published in June 2004.

"Vanderbilt's Folly" Is Fun

The hot and sticky summer Saturday had Tom, my cycling companion, and me questioning our choice of times to try a new trail. Instead of a single track winding through shady hardwoods, we had selected an abandoned 8.5-mile section of the Pennsylvania Turnpike from Breezewood east into

The First Frontier

Fulton County. Leaving U.S. Route 30 at the Ramada Inn of Breezewood, we drove through an unimproved parking area to a short, eroded access. Traveling back almost forty years in three hundred feet, we dropped down onto two strips of seemingly narrow concrete, fringed with wayside weeds. No diesel-engine snarl here, just the steady drone of locusts on a steamy afternoon. To the left was the trailhead: a line of Jersey barriers stretching across the roadway with a break just wide enough for a person and bicycle.

How highway design has changed over the past sixty years! Only ten feet of medial strip separated the pairs of lanes. At the Rays Hill and Sideling Hill Tunnels, the four lanes merged into two—one for eastbound traffic, the other for westbound. This day, however, these twenty-four-foot-wide concrete strips offered a surprisingly intimate and pleasant cycling experience despite the afternoon heat. (Fat-tired bikes are recommended, though, because of the crumbling concrete.) Trees, shrubs and wayside plants, no longer kept at bay by right-of-way maintenance, shaded long sections. Constructed to a grade of 3 percent or less, the trail's hills are no more challenging than a rail-trail's. And there is plenty of room to ride, enjoy the Buchanan State Forest scenery and ponder the transportation history here.

Back in the 1880s, William H. Vanderbilt was upset that the Pennsylvania Railroad was competing with his New York City & Hudson River Railroad. Vanderbilt teamed with Pittsburgh industrialists, who were unhappy with PRR freight rates, to start developing the Southern Pennsylvania Railroad. Work on what became known as "Vanderbilt's Folly" stopped in 1885 after a loss of dozens of workers' lives and an expenditure of $10 million. Pennsylvania's legacy, however, was a roadbed and partially excavated tunnels through a number of ridges including Rays Hill and Sideling Hill. When civil engineers began considering where to place the corridor for America's first superhighway in the mid-1930s, the old Southern Pennsylvania right-of-way was selected.

Construction of the initial 160-mile Pennsylvania Turnpike reflected a number of radical changes in highway design. Cross streets, railroad crossings and traffic lights were eliminated; access was limited to on- and off-ramps. Curves were limited in radius and banked to facilitate higher speeds. Grades were kept to 3 percent. There were two twelve-foot lanes in each direction, separated by a ten-foot median and flanked by ten-foot shoulders. Actual construction of the initial section took only about fourteen months, and the Pennsylvania Turnpike opened in September 1940.

Pennsylvania's Allegheny Mountains

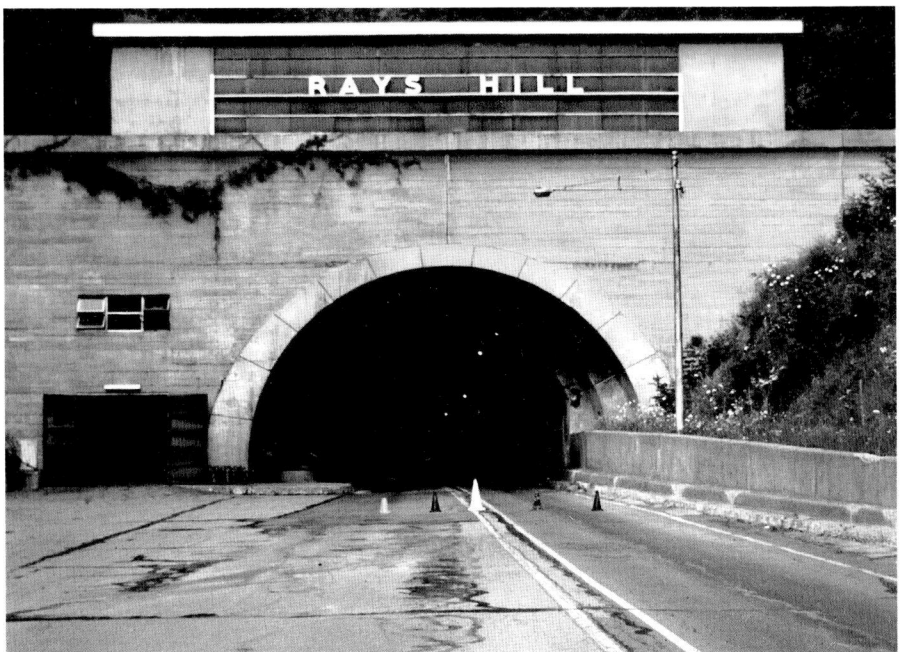

The Rays Hill Tunnel of the Pennsylvania Turnpike in 1973, shortly after its abandonment. *Photograph by Mitchell Dakelman.*

The Rays Hill and Sideling Hill Tunnels proved to be major bottlenecks, though, because they'd only been excavated to accommodate two lanes of traffic—one in either direction. So an eleven-mile stretch of the original turnpike, containing these two tunnels, was bypassed in 1968 after engineers concluded that it made more sense to build new highway than to expand the two tunnels or dig two new ones. For thirty-three years, the abandoned section sat largely idle, used only for storage and the testing of drivers, equipment, road surfaces and signs. Finally, however, the abandoned section was sold for one dollar to the Bedford-based Southern Alleghenies Conservancy in 2001.

Now the two tunnels are the most interesting features of this trail. But bring a light if you don't want to grope your way through. Upon entering the Ray's Hill Tunnel, the other end—seven-tenths of a mile away—looks like a narrow horizontal strip of reflective tape. (The road rises toward the middle of the tunnel, blocking most of the light from the far portal.) No light is visible upon entering the 1.3-mile Sideling Hill Tunnel. As dark, cool sanctuaries on a bright, hot day, the tunnels are a big hit with riders.

The First Frontier

Even in its primitive condition, this is a trail worth riding. Its corridor offers more than 120 years of heritage, its features still showcase highway engineering of the mid-twentieth century and today it is one of America's unique multiple-use trails.

First published in August 2005.

PART V

Leisure in the Alleghenies

Gilded, Thrilling and Delicious

Seemingly incongruous with the concepts of the Alleghenies as a bloody battleground, a barrier to development, a challenging workplace and a rough place to live is the fact that these ridges have long been a recreational haven. As harsh a home as they have been for struggling immigrants, the Alleghenies also nurtured and preserved cultural heritage and holiday traditions by keeping ethnic groups cloistered. Some of our nation's wealthiest men—Andrew Carnegie, Henry Clay Frick and Charles Schwab among them—came to these cool, verdant hills to escape the sweltering, sooty conditions of late nineteenth-century urban life.

The leisure legacy of Pennsylvania's Allegheny Mountains is surprisingly rich, amazingly extant and expressed in a variety of ways that are not only fascinating but also invigorating, even delectable, to experience.

The Lure of Angling's Heritage

They line the banks, young and old, male and female. Some take their fishing way too seriously, casting nasty looks whenever an upstream line crosses theirs; others don't take theirs seriously enough, laughing and splashing and spooking every fish in the hole. The opening day of trout season is one of our special days—a rite of spring, a time with family and friends, a day of snags and line snarls and success catching naïve stocked trout. Fly fishers tend to stay in the background on opening day, sharing in the joy of a fresh season but eagerly anticipating the time ahead, when the opening-day throngs with their canned corn and neon-colored paste will be gone. Later, while sending a stone fly arcing into that same hole, the fly fisher may consider the opening-day spectacle and think, "Now this is true trout fishing—the way it's been done for hundreds of years."

The fly fisher would be both right and wrong. Ken Reinard of Lititz fly-fishes the way it was done hundreds of years ago. But when he steps onto a stream bank, he is as far removed from modern fly fishers as they are from the canned-corn crowd. His dark-brown wool frock coat has tails to the knees. Underneath, he wears a light-brown weskit, knee breeches and charcoal-gray stockings. A black broad-brimmed hat and black square-toed shoes complete his fishing outfit. As "Ye Olde Colonial Angler of 1770," Reinard has found a way to combine two of his passions: eighteenth-century reenacting and fly-fishing.

"One must be of noble and free birth if we are to continue this conversation," Reinard said as he kidded the forty people who attended his program at the Somerset Historical Center. Angling—which means "to hook"—was a

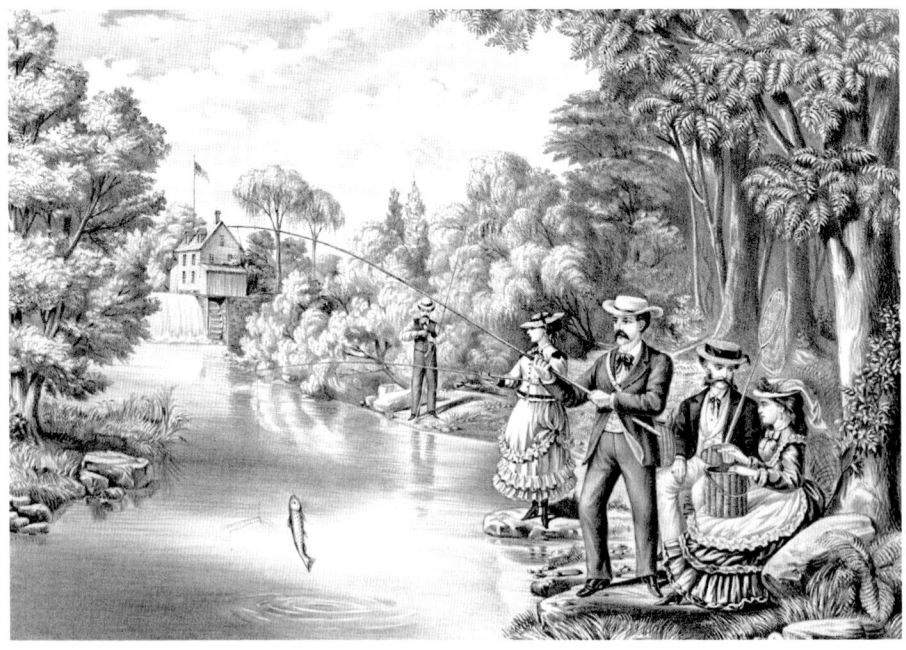

An 1870 lithograph originally published by John Walsh & Co. of New York, illustrating the trout-fishing social scene. *Prints and Photographs Division, Library of Congress.*

The First Frontier

sport for nobility only from the fifteenth to eighteenth centuries, according to Reinard. Only nobles could afford the tackle, which was all hand-made and very expensive.

There were no reels. Rods were fifteen or twenty feet long and made of various hollowed woods in six or seven sections lashed or joined together. Line was made from braided horsehair and fixed to the end of the rod. Flies were tied to hooks made from needles and "skittered" on top of the water. Landing a trout on a barbless hook with a twenty-foot, reel-less rod was a real challenge. The proper technique was to keep the trout directly under the rod tip until it tired. If the fish ran away from the bank, the fisher threw the rod in, waited for the fish to tire and then sent his "gilly" to retrieve both the rod and the fish. A "gilly" was a sportsman's attendant who handled both the equipment and the fish. After all, the fisher wouldn't risk soiling or ruining his or her fine clothes. In those days, angling was a true social event that often included a sumptuous, creek-side repast. Because both lords and ladies participated, fishers dressed for fashion, not function.

This sport always has been enjoyed as readily by women as by men. In fact, the oldest surviving written work on fishing, *The Treatyse of Fysshynge Wyth Angle*, published in 1496, was authored by Dame Juliana Bemers, an English nun. That a nun would write about fishing should not be surprising. Fishing was a spiritual experience, a time to observe nature and reflect on the wonders of creation. The priority was not on catching as many trout as possible, according to Reinard, but rather, "What did we learn today? What did God show us?"

Today, the gillies are gone. The tackle has evolved. But sunlight still reflects from the riffles, the mayfly still perches on an arched leaf, the stream still playfully swashes and many of us still know the spiritual experience of trout fishing.

First published in April 2004.

The Shape of Our Musical Heritage

The overcast December Sunday's subdued light suited the gray woolen uniforms of the Confederate soldiers, seated to the left of the altar within the Mount Union Church near Rockwood. To the altar's right sat men in Union blue.

Pennsylvania's Allegheny Mountains

"Whether you wear blue or gray or neither, you are welcome in this place of peace," pronounced the Reverend James Monticue, who then invited the soldiers to shake hands as a sign of peace during the Christmas service. This was a combination reenactment and worship service emblematic of Christmas-truce events that took place during the Civil War. Not only were the church and the uniforms circa 1861, so was the Christmas carol sung a cappella in four-part harmony by a group of eight people:

While shepherds watched their flocks by night,
All seated on the ground,
The angel of the Lord came down,
And glory shone around.

The words of this carol are familiar to many today, but the melody sung this day probably would sound strange to most ears. Were you to check the music, you would notice odd-looking notes. While the usual stems and flags

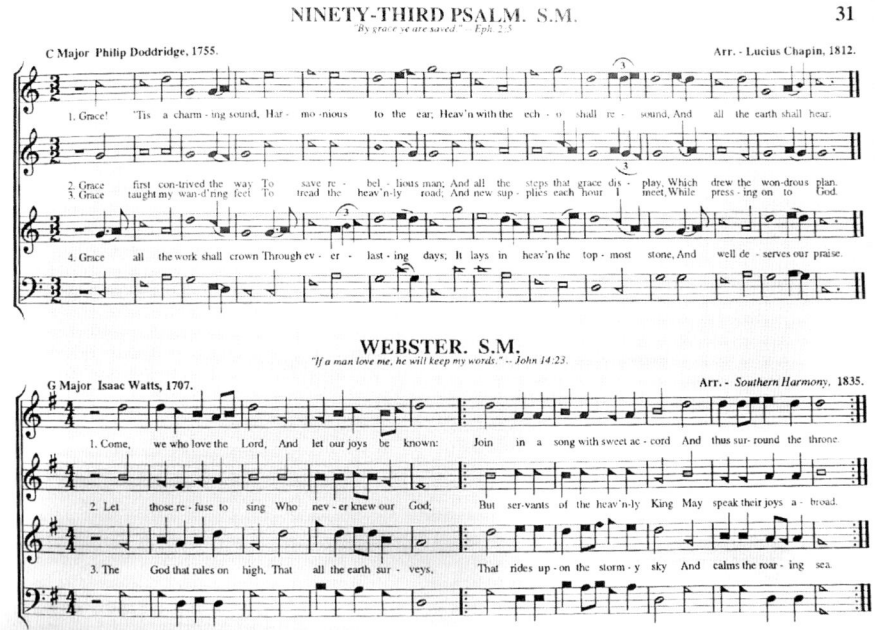

Two examples of shape-note music published in *The Sacred Harp* songbook. *Sacred Harp Publishing Company, Inc.*

The First Frontier

are present, only some of the notes have elliptical heads; other note heads are shaped like rectangles, triangles and diamonds. These are called "shape notes," and they record America's first music.

In the late eighteenth and early nineteenth centuries, a new nation was creating its own identity, including its first indigenous music. This early American music tended toward short tunes rather than European-influenced classical compositions and was mostly sacred, often using lyrics written by the great hymnologists such as Isaac Watts and Charles Wesley. Because this music was sung in churches by people who couldn't read music, composers and tune book publishers developed a simple four-note system that tied the pitch to the shape of the note: The "fa" note had a triangular head, "sol" was elliptical, "la" was rectangular and "mi" was diamond-shaped. Placing shape notes on the five-lined music staff enabled singers to determine the pitch relative to the preceding notes. Tune books, containing hundreds of sacred songs written with shape notes, spread this music across the country during much of the nineteenth century.

While shape-note music fell out of favor in the North, it became deeply entrenched in the rural churches of the South, where it still is sung. Interestingly, over the past forty years this folk tradition has experienced a revival nationwide—especially in university communities. Today, people of all walks of life—including many non-Christians—are discovering the joy of singing early American shape-note music, which often is referred to as "Sacred Harp" singing. (*The Sacred Harp*, published in 1844, is the most popular of the shape-note tune books. The phrase "sacred harp" refers to the unaccompanied human voice.)

This music is sung to one another, not performed for an audience. People gather and sit in a "hollow square" facing one another; trebles, altos, tenors and basses each occupying their own side of the square. The first time through, the song sounds like so much babble because each part is being sung to the names of the shape-notes: "Sol-fa-fa-fa-la-sol-sol-la…" Then singers shift to the words, and the music's dynamic energy erupts. Sometimes lively, other times mournful, often sung in a minor key to lyrics that tend to focus on life's struggles and the hope of salvation, shape-note music is raw and emotive with captivating harmonies. Its lack of sophistication is its attraction. Singing well is less important than singing fervently.

Just as it has been in recent years across the country, this musical tradition is reemerging in our region today. Sacred Harp singings occur each month at Mount Union Church and at University Mennonite Church in State College.

Consider experiencing shape-note singing. You don't need Christian faith, musical knowledge or a great voice—just the desire to make joyful noise.

First published in December 2007.

Holidays of Early Advent

A white-bearded, red-robed man strolls the halls of the Northern Cambria Catholic School amid the din of excited elementary students, but he may not be the fellow you are picturing. This man wears a peaked bishop's miter and carries a tall staff. As he distributes his treats, he asks questions of the kids, testing their knowledge of the church and scripture. Saint Nicholas makes an appearance at the Nicktown school every year around December 6, which is Saint Nicholas's Day in Catholic and Orthodox churches. He also shows up at the local parish's annual covered-dish dinner and hands out gold-wrapped chocolate coins to the kids.

"It's a German tradition and we are a German parish," said the Reverend Job Foote, OSB, pastor of St. Nicholas Catholic Church. Parishioners there also practice another old Saint Nicholas tradition. Before going to bed on December 5, the kids put their shoes outside their bedrooms. They awaken the next morning to find their shoes filled with sweets and small gifts if they've been good—or twigs if they haven't.

A beloved bishop in the fourth century (AD), Nicholas was called "the Wonderworker" for the many miracles attributed to him. The tradition of placing gold-wrapped chocolate coins on children's bedroom window sills or in their shoes can be traced to his practice of secretly giving his inheritance to the needy. Of course Saint Nicholas influenced our American Christmas traditions, which took off in directions of their own after Clement Moore penned "The Night Before Christmas" and Thomas Nast drew the first Santa Claus in a mid-nineteenth-century cartoon in *Harper's Weekly*.

In European tradition, however, Nicholas is one of three "parading figures" that were used to celebrate early Advent. There also was Saint Barbara, whose day is December 4. Barbara was a martyr of the third-century church, killed by her own father because of her faith. According to church lore, afterward, as the saint's father was traveling home, he was struck and killed by lightning. That connection with fire and explosion made Saint Barbara the patron saint of field artillery and explains why many U.S. Army

The First Frontier

and Marine Corps field artillery units hold formal dinners on December 4. Central European villagers celebrated Saint Barbara's Day by wandering the evening streets, dressed in a white cloak and wearing masks of a woman's face and wigs of long hair topped with wreaths. They carried switches for bad children and baskets of fruit and nuts for good ones. In one enduring tradition, people cut cherry tree shoots on Saint Barbara's Day and put them in vases; they bloom by Christmas and symbolize hope and good fortune.

Saint Lucy's Day is December 13 and traditionally marks the beginning of the Christmas season in Sweden, where she is the patron saint. As Santa Lucia, she also is revered in Sicily, where she was martyred for being a Christian in the early fourth century. Traditionally in Sweden, the youngest girl in the family proceeds around the house, wearing a headdress comprised of a wreath and candles (now electronic) and serving sweet buns and coffee. In Sicily, women make cuccia—a sweet dish of wheat berries, chocolate, sugar and milk—and have their kids distribute it to neighbors and friends.

While traces of these Advent holiday traditions still can be found here, they are disappearing as each generation grows more distant from its immigrant ancestors and as American traditions increasingly supplant those of the Old World. Let's not lose them entirely. For in a gold-wrapped chocolate coin sitting in a child's shoe, in a sprig of cherry blooming on Christmas Day or in a bowl of cuccia, there is more than heritage; there are nuggets of truth about the real reason for Advent season.

First published in December 2003.

Mitchell Day

If April 1 arrives and no union coal miners gather around pitchers, pigs and pierogies to celebrate Mitchell Day, our region will have lost something precious—and a great party. If you've not heard of Mitchell Day, then you've not spent much time around coal miners. In United Mine Workers of America labor agreements, Mitchell Day is a holiday. But for union miners, it's more than just a paid day off.

"Mitchell Day is something like a holy day to the miner," said Toby Fleegle, president of UMWA Local 6410, based in Central City, Somerset County, and a fourth-generation coal miner.

The day is named for John Mitchell, an early president of the UMWA, who negotiated the first eight-hour workday during the Great Anthracite Strike of 1902. We take the "right" of a reasonable workday for granted today, but before the eight-hour workday law was passed during the New Deal in the 1930s, coal operators and most other employers didn't provide it willingly. So Mitchell's success at the negotiating table was no small achievement, and if you ask most miners why they celebrate Mitchell Day, that's what they talk about.

Mitchell's greater accomplishment was to bring immigrant miners into the union. Undereducated and speaking different languages, early mine workers stuck to their own ethnic groups and didn't like one another. Union organizers overcame miners' differences by pointing out that roof falls and mine explosions didn't discriminate. In the ten years of Mitchell's presidency, from 1898 to 1908, UMWA membership exploded from 33,000 to 260,000. "United we stand, divided we fall, a wrong to one is a wrong to all!" became the UMWA credo that created one of the nation's largest unions and eventually spawned the United Steelworkers of America and the American Federation of Labor and Congress of Industrial Organizations (AFL-CIO).

The UMWA's success didn't happen quickly or easily. Mine operators, such as the Berwind-White Coal Company of Philadelphia, which had thirteen mines in northern Somerset and southern Cambria counties, fought unionization with a passion and wielded their biggest weapon—control over worker housing—without compassion. Miners suspected of union activity were fired, and their families immediately were ejected from company housing. During long, violent strikes in the 1920s, Berwind forced families to endure harsh Allegheny winters in tents. It wasn't until organized labor convinced Congress to pass labor rights bills, during the New Deal, and World War II created a demand for coal that thrust all other issues aside that the UMWA was able to organize mines throughout Appalachia.

Meanwhile, mine workers were creating a new culture that fused "Union" with family and ethnicity. Mitchell Day became an annual celebration of that culture—a day when miners gathered at their Local or social club, ate heartily, drank spiritedly and—in colorful mining jargon—talked with one another, toasted the UMWA and roasted coal operators.

"It was a big holiday for us at home—like a Christmas or an Easter at my house," recalled Frank Romus, a past president of Local 6410, whose father also was a miner. Now retired—"pensioneers" as they're known in the coal fields—Romus and Fleegle were sitting at one end of the U-shaped bar of the Slovak

The First Frontier

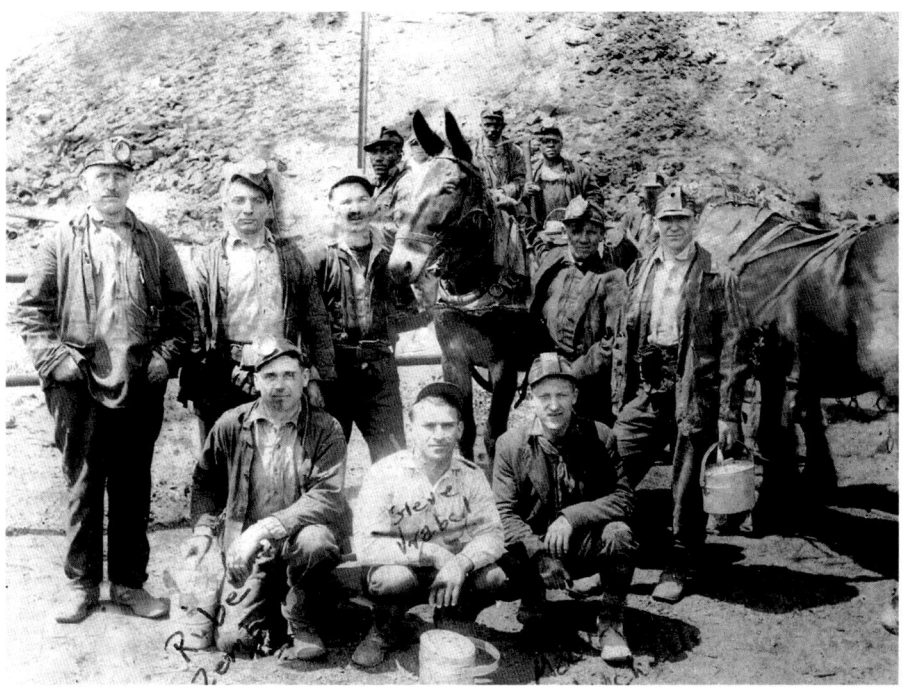

Coal miners of various ethnicities with their mules and lunch buckets circa 1920. *Coal and Coke Heritage Center, Pennsylvania State University–Fayette, Eberly Campus, Hunchuck Collection.*

Educational Club in Windber on Mitchell Day 2003. Downstairs, women were preparing a classic Mitchell Day meal: holupki (pigs in a blanket), haluski (cabbage and noodles) and pierogies with nut roll or poppy seed roll for dessert.

Mitchell Day celebrations are getting harder to find here. Today, there are fewer active union miners in all of Pennsylvania than were working in Cambria County alone just twenty-five years ago—and the pensioneers are passing away. We should keep Mitchell Day alive as a regional day of labor celebration. We could gather at local clubs, eat some picrogies and listen to old miners talk of gassy mines and strikes, of colorful characters, of wives and mothers making good homes through hard work and inventiveness and of the struggle for a better life. Remember that these are the stories of our ancestors, neighbors and communities. This is part of our heritage, too.

Would miners mind sharing Mitchell Day? I don't think so. They just might expect us to buy the first round.

First published in April 2003.

Lent Takes the Pagan to Church

We talk about walking on eggshells but imagine writing on them. Imagine tracing intricate geometric forms or figures of deer, storks, fish, wheat, crosses and crowns of thorns on that hard, brittle, curved canvas and framing the figures in rich colors of yellow, green, orange, brown and purple. Then imagine that you are selecting the specific forms, figures and colors because they will have meaning for a special someone. Now look at a pysanka—a Ukrainian Easter egg—and see how your imaginings compare to the actual folk art. Of course, thousands of people within our region have no trouble imagining pysanky at all. They display them proudly in their homes as treasured family heirlooms, gifts from loved ones or creations of their own. Many of these people are Ukrainian Orthodox, and during the Lenten season their ethnic heritage in the shape of these beautiful symbolic eggs earns some well-deserved attention.

Creating pysanky (the name comes from the Ukrainian verb meaning "to write") is an ancient folk art in the Ukraine. Originally, early Ukrainians considered the egg a symbol of fertility. Enhancing its symbolism with decorations and giving the pysanka to someone became an important rite of spring. With the introduction of Christianity, pysanka "writers" started to include religious symbolism. This pagan rite of spring became an Orthodox observance during Lent. Women would spend Lenten evenings richly detailing their unique creations and keeping them hidden until Easter Sunday. On Easter the pysanky would be brought to church together with traditional foods in a basket that was blessed by the priest. Then the eggs would be exchanged with family and friends—given with the traditional greeting "Christ has risen," accepted with the traditional response "He is risen indeed."

Traditional Lenten and Easter foods also reflect the intertwining of cultural and religious roots. Kielbasa, according to the Ukrainian Orthodox, was originally a ritual food eaten to commune with the god of the wild boar. Now it's one of the traditional foods blessed by the priest and an essential ingredient in some versions of Easter soup. This season's blending of pagan and Christian elements even extends to the names "Easter" and "Lent," which aren't found in the Bible. Both are thought to have been derived from ancient words for spring. Easter may have come from the Anglo-Saxon goddess of spring Eostre (who was associated with eggs and the hare). Lent was drawn from a Teutonic word that meant the

The First Frontier

spring season. Christian references to Lent date back 1,800 years, however, and from that earliest reference through the present, Christians have embraced the Lenten or Paschal (a name applied to Jesus but borrowed from the Jewish name of the lamb sacrificed at Passover) season as a time of reflection, penitence and self-denial.

Sadly, ethnic Easter customs are disappearing in our region. While there are still at least fourteen parishes listed in our region by the Ukrainian Orthodox Church of the United States of America (we have the largest concentration of parishes in the country), priests with whom I spoke said that their congregations are shrinking, aging and no longer observing pysanka traditions, for example. Fortunately, there still are opportunities to experience pysanka writing—or even own some examples of this ancient, symbolic folk art. Johnstown's Bottle Works Ethnic Arts Center and the Somerset Historical Center occasionally offer displays and pysanky workshops, and Saints Peter and Paul Ukrainian Orthodox Church in Carnegie, near Pittsburgh, holds a huge annual sale of pysanky during Lent. Kielbasa, fortunately, is readily available—as are recipes for Easter soup.

So flavor this Lenten season with ethnic traditions and don't be surprised if these blended, pagan-religious customs heighten your spirituality.

First published in March 2006.

A Great Old Story Gets New Wrinkles

Johnstown and Memorial Day will be linked forever. For it was on that holiday in 1889 that a fateful rainfall began, according to Reverend David Beal in *Through the Johnstown Flood*:

> *After nightfall the clouds grew heavier, hanging nearer the earth, and at 9 o'clock a gentle drizzling rain set in, which, after 11 o'clock, was followed by an unprecedented outpour.*

Inch upon inch of rain fell that night and the following day, filling a mountain resort's reservoir to overflowing, fourteen miles up the Little Conemaugh River.

The South Fork Dam had originally been constructed to feed water into the Pennsylvania Main Line Canal, whose Western Division started in Johnstown and ended in Pittsburgh. Once the canal was purchased by the Pennsylvania Railroad in the mid-1850s, the dam was abandoned and its reservoir largely drained. Then in 1879 the property was purchased by Benjamin Ruff who, together with fifteen other shareholders, formed the South Fork Fishing and Hunting Club. They repaired the dam, stocked the reservoir—which they named "Lake Conemaugh"—with game fish and added some "improvements" such as a fish screen in front of the spillway to keep fish in the lake. As a summer resort for the elite of Pittsburgh, which already was well on its way to becoming the nation's industrial capital, the South Fork club's membership list carried names still readily recognizable today: Andrew Carnegie, Henry Clay Frick, Philander Knox, Robert Pitcairn and Andrew Mellon among them.

While no expense was spared to make the South Fork club a comfortable and delightful place for members, the same could not be said for the dam itself. Ruff and the other shareholders had made haphazard repairs to the old dam, simply filling in the breech with an assortment of materials to the original height. The old discharge pipes, removed by a previous owner, were not replaced. The shoddily repaired dam, lack of discharge pipes and debris-

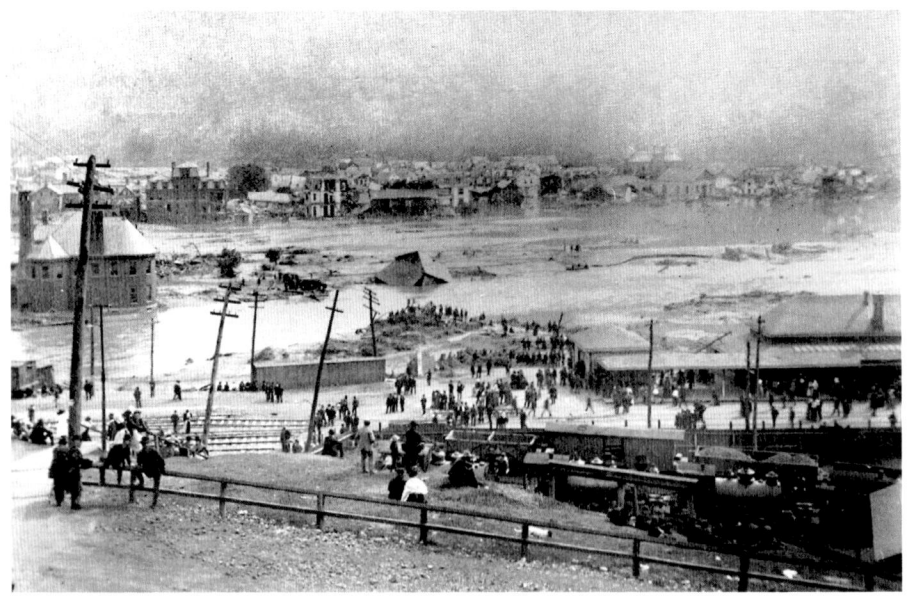

Downtown Johnstown shortly after the 1889 Flood. The Little Conemaugh riverbed is on the near side of the building on the left. *National Park Service, Johnstown Flood National Memorial.*

The First Frontier

clogging fish screen became fatal factors during the unusually intense storm event that had begun on Memorial Day and continued into the next day.

When the South Fork Dam suddenly gave way just after 3:00 p.m. on May 31, 1889, it released a quantity and velocity of water into the Little Conemaugh River valley that was the equivalent of thirty-five to forty-five minutes' worth of Niagara Falls. The resulting wall of water and debris slammed into the Conemaugh Valley, scoured the center of Johnstown, and killed more than 2,200 people. The calamity was the 9/11 of the nineteenth century and captured worldwide attention. While there was public outrage over the apparent liability of the South Fork club, the courts ruled the disaster an act of God. However, the intense news coverage prompted an unprecedented outpouring of public charity and made a household name of Clara Barton and the American Red Cross. So notorious was this event that more than a century later people around the world still know of the Great Johnstown Flood.

You know about it, too, but when's the last time you experienced Johnstown and its history? If your answer is "Never" or "It's been awhile," consider spending part of your Memorial Day weekend there. Far from being dry and depressing, this is a gripping and inspiring story for the ages with plot elements ranging from the elitist naiveté of the South Fork Fishing and Hunting Club to the horrific carnage, dramatic rescues, heart-warming world response and resolute spirit that brought recovery.

Some of the best first-person material came from the Reverend David Beale. Beale was the pastor of the Presbyterian Church downtown, survived the flood himself and supervised an emergency morgue established in his church. His *Through the Johnstown Flood* is one of the most respected eyewitness accounts of the disaster, and just a few years ago the Johnstown Area Heritage Association (JAHA) received a large collection of Beale materials, including thirty handwritten diaries, a morgue book, eighty photographs of flood destruction and personal letters.

In addition to the Johnstown Flood Museum, which is located in the former library building donated by Carnegie following the flood, JAHA also operates a Johnstown Children's Museum with flood-related exhibits. The National Park Service operates the Johnstown Flood Memorial at the site of the former dam and reservoir.

Experience this story as these facilities skillfully tell it, and you may start linking Johnstown and your Memorial Day for years to come.

First published in May 2007.

The Alleghenies' Gilded Age

A television news director I once worked for often said that the story can be at right angles to the event, meaning that a good news story may not be the obvious one (although we reporters suspected that he just wanted to justify boring assignments). His truism came to mind during a guided stroll at the Johnstown Flood National Memorial near St. Michael. The National Park Service offers these strolls as a way to interpret 1880s life at the South Fork Hunting and Fishing Club—before its dam failed and caused the 1889 Johnstown Flood.

Now, I'm not suggesting that the story of how Pittsburgh's wealthy spent their leisure time compares with the story of one of the worst natural disasters in U.S. history. The 1889 Flood story is one of gripping drama, almost unimaginable tragedy, individual heroism and spiritual triumph.

Overshadowed, however—at right angles to the flood story—are engaging accounts of the brief, eight-year period when the Gilded Age came into the Allegheny Mountains and relaxed at Lake Conemaugh. After the South Fork club opened in 1881, Pittsburgh's wealthy would travel via Pennsylvania Railroad to South Fork Station, where they would board a hackney for the 2.5-mile ride to the club. The ride, which must have been beautiful, took them upstream along the South Fork of the Little Conemaugh River, across the spillway on a wooden bridge, atop the breast of the dam, around the lakeshore along a wooded hillside and, finally, to the capacious, three-story, wood-framed Victorian clubhouse.

The carriage path along the hillside remains, and the park service guide takes visitors there from the South Abutment parking lot up a gentle, grassy slope banked with jewelweed and onto a graveled greenway through the hardwoods. As we walk, the guide pulls crisp, black-and-white photos from a file folder that open a fascinating window into that time at this place.

Historians knew that Henry Clay Frick, Andrew Mellon, Philander Knox, Henry Phipps Jr. and Andrew Carnegie were members of the South Fork club. They knew how much money was spent repairing the dam and why the dam failed. But historians didn't know much about life at the exclusive club—until the marvelous photographs of club member Louis Semple Clarke surfaced in a New England attic in the 1980s. Clarke, an avid photographer, delighted in capturing images of the club's people and activities. Dozens of his high-quality negatives survived. Both sailboats and small steamboats cruised the water of Lake Conemaugh. Evidently, there

The First Frontier

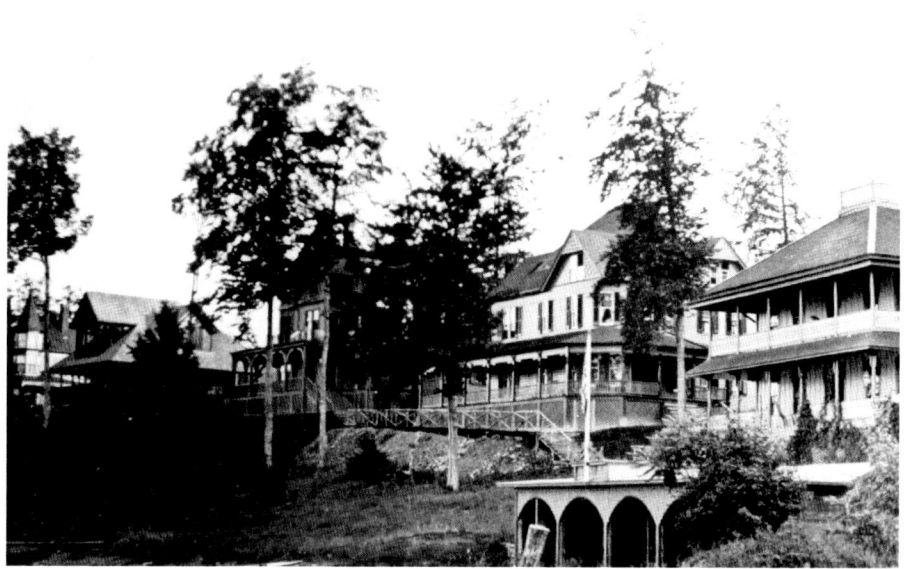

Victorian cottages at Lake Conemaugh during the days of the South Fork Fishing and Hunting Club. *Photograph by Louis Semple Clark, National Park Service, Virginia A. Soule Collection.*

were a number of plays performed for the entertainment of the guests, based on the number of images showing mostly young people in a variety of costumes. Other photographs show people lounging on swings and furniture on the spacious, wraparound porches of the large Victorian "cottages" that lined the lakeshore.

Park service strolls do include some dramatic elements of the flood story, such as the desperate efforts of workers to save the dam and to warn the populace downriver. But this gentle, cerebral exercise is intended to convey the soothing rhythms of the good life enjoyed here by the privileged few. It ends on the generous front porch of the South Fork clubhouse. Afterward, some visitors view the video *A Victorian Summer* and look at the eleven surviving buildings from the period. Others go to the visitors' center or on into Johnstown to learn more about the flood.

Set aside a couple of hours for the stroll and the remainder of the day to learn about the 1889 Flood, and you'll have an experience that leaves a lifelong impression. For this is a fascinating story set at right angles to an extraordinary event.

First published in August 2004.

Classic Amusement

Even in the amusement park—that never-never land constantly appealing to our eternal youthfulness with faster coasters and splashier water rides—age is venerated. The eight-thousand-member American Coaster Enthusiasts organization, for example, is often asked about the oldest operating roller coaster. There's also a National Amusement Park Historical Association (NAPHA) that lists the world's fifty oldest amusement parks still operating in their original locations. Disney and Busch may dominate the theme parks. Cedar Point may be a mecca for coaster addicts. But for amusement park heritage, people flock to the classic parks of Pennsylvania's Alleghenies: Idlewild Park near Ligonier, Lakemont Park in Altoona and Kennywood Park in West Mifflin.

Idlewild is the third-oldest park still operating in the United States and the eleventh oldest in the world. Lakemont is the nation's sixteenth-oldest, while Kennywood ranks nineteenth. All three were established by transportation companies looking for ways to generate new traffic—especially on weekends when their rolling stock was too still. The coal-hauling Ligonier Valley Railroad created Idlewild for "picnic purposes or pleasure grounds" in 1878. Originally a campground offering fishing, boating and picnicking in its beautiful Loyalhanna Valley setting, Idlewild started adding other attractions in the 1930s. Lakemont and Kennywood both began as picnic parks at the end of urban trolley lines. Typical of many "trolley parks" of the period, Lakemont and Kennywood added rides, lights and sounds to attract more patrons.

Most coaster enthusiasts can tell you about Lakemont's biggest claim to fame: its Leap-the-Dips is the world's oldest operating roller coaster, opening in 1902 and still featuring unique side-mounted wheel cars. Kennywood's claim of being "America's Finest Traditional Park" is supported by the fact that the park has been voted the "favorite traditional amusement park" of NAPHA members for every year except one since 1987, dominating Cedar Point and Blackpool Pleasure Beach in the United Kingdom among others. A glance at NAPHA's list of classic rides shows why Kennywood is so beloved by traditional-park enthusiasts. The Old Mill there is the world's oldest operating water ride, opening in 1901. Its Jack Rabbit coaster is the seventh-oldest in the world, while its twin-tracked Racer ranks seventeenth. Auto Race, Tumble Bug, Flying Coaster, Noah's Ark and Whip all are Kennywood rides listed on NAPHA's list of nationally recognized classics.

The First Frontier

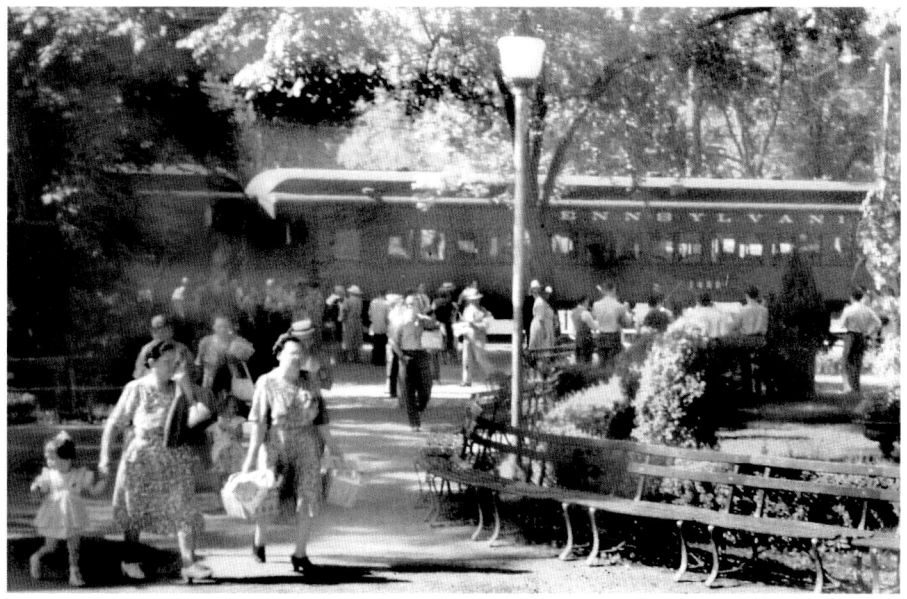

People disembark from a Pennsylvania Railroad train for a day at Idlewild Park in this undated photo. *Idlewild Park Archives.*

Idlewild also gets national recognition for its Caterpillar—one of only four that still have their canopies—and its Whip.

More than just the setting for classic rides, though, these parks have a cultured look that newer parks just can't duplicate. Massive shade trees sheltering benches and generous, landscaped lawns flanking walkways show why such places first became known as amusement "parks." Vintage well-kept wood-frame buildings with turn-of-the-century ambiance house concessions, arcades and midway games. Lakes seem indigenous to the landscape.

A closer look at NAPHA's list of classic rides will reveal yet another reason why our region's amusement park heritage is so rich: the name of Traver Engineering of Beaver Falls. Harry Traver already had made a name for himself in the amusement ride industry when he found his way to the Ohio River Valley in 1919. Within five years, his thirteen-acre complex would become the world's largest producer of amusement park rides. Traver-built rides entertained patrons in Paris, Bombay, Shanghai, Berlin, Vienna, Buenos Aires and New Zealand, leading him to boast that the sun never set on his work. Nor has the sun set on his rides today. While Traver lost his business in the Great Depression, his Auto Race and Tumble Bug still operate at Kennywood and his Caterpillar continues to undulate at Idlewild.

Amid the flash and dash of today's amusement park industry, our classic parks are proving that entertainment can be ageless and heritage can be thrilling.

First published in May 2003.

Try to Resist This Taste of Our Heritage

My first bite: chunks of pineapple, vanilla ice cream, banana and whipped cream. *Oh, that's sweet.* Here comes the second: chocolate syrup, chocolate ice cream, banana, whipped cream and chopped nuts. *Just this side of decadent.* Now the third: a slice of strawberry, strawberry ice cream, banana and whipped cream. *Ahh, nirvana. What's Joe saying? I'd better write this down. Can't he see that I'm trying to do some serious eat—er—research here?*

"Ice Cream Joe" Greubel and I are sitting in a Valley Dairy Restaurant at the corner of Chestnut and Jefferson Streets in downtown Latrobe—arguably the spiritual home for the "All-American Banana Split," as it's listed on Valley Dairy's menu. Latrobe's now-departed Tassell's Drug Store—once located mere blocks from where I'm sitting—was the banana split's birthplace. There in 1904 a twenty-three-year-old soda jerk named David Strickler first halved a banana, scooped in vanilla, chocolate and strawberry ice cream, dribbled on toppings, sprinkled chopped nuts, plopped dollops of whipped cream on each scoop then capped everything with a cherry. Before long, students from nearby St. Vincent College, undeterred by a ten-cent price, were discovering Strickler's new ice cream concoction. Since many of the students were from out of state, word of the banana split quickly spread nationwide.

Oh, there are pretenders—other communities have entered claims to being the banana split's home. But thanks to the work of a local newspaper columnist named Jack George and Strickler's own documentation, provided in the 1950s to the network TV program *I've Got a Secret*, Latrobe's preeminence in the banana split realm stands as proud as the American flag that Valley Dairy plants atop the dish's middle peak.

Tassell's and Strickler are gone now. But Ice Cream Joe, Valley Dairy's president, is committed to perpetuating Latrobe's banana split legacy. The cause could not be in better hands. Ice cream imbues the life of Joseph E. Greubel—who is actually Ice Cream Joe Jr. His father, Joseph F. Greubel, the founder of Valley Dairy, was the original Ice Cream Joe—he

The First Frontier

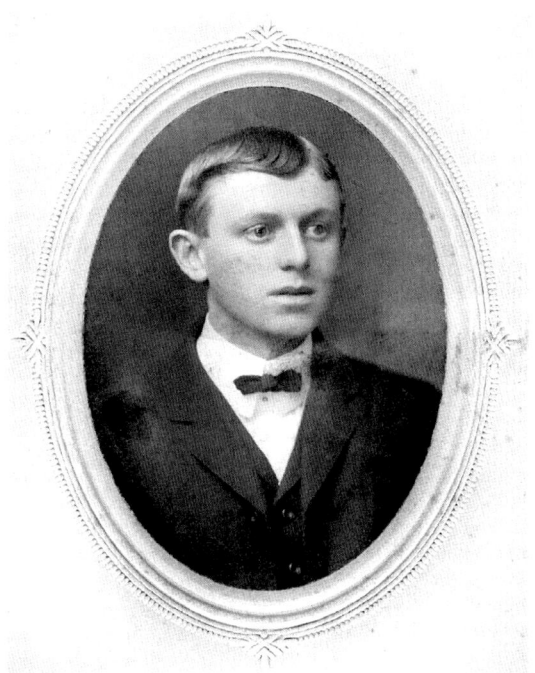

David Strickler, who invented the banana split in 1904 at Tassell's Drug Store in Latrobe, Pennsylvania. *Latrobe Area Historical Society*

even had the name trademarked. It's Joseph F.'s picture that is so familiar to Valley Dairy patrons: white-haired, with glasses occasionally perched on the tip of his nose. In one photograph he's turning the crank on an ice cream freezer marked with the date 1884—the year his grandfather, Joseph A. Greubel, became the first commercial ice cream producer in Westmoreland County. Valley Dairy remains a Greubel family affair. The current Ice Cream Joe's wife and two of his daughters are officers in the company, which oversees eleven family-styled restaurants in eight counties, plus the Fairview Dairy of Windber, which makes and distributes Valley Dairy Ice Cream to five states.

As I concentrate on preventing melted ice cream from sloshing off the ends of my long but shallow metal dish, Joe talks excitedly about the national awards for ice cream excellence won by the company and about the upcoming annual Ice Screamers Convention in Lancaster. As my strawberry, chocolate and vanilla ice creams blend, their toppings becoming ingredients in the soup, Joe talks of the banana split's 100th birthday celebration that was held in Latrobe and of the community's intentions to hold annual celebrations during July, which is National Ice Cream Month.

Of course, special events aren't needed to celebrate this sumptuous regional product. Given the banana split's ubiquity, you can "research" this taste of home wherever you are, whenever you want. And if anyone suggests that you are overindulging, look them straight in the eye and inform them that you are simply experiencing your heritage.

Oooh, this last bite's the best: melted ice cream with chunks of strawberry, pineapple, banana and the cherry!

First published in July 2005.

Appendix

Exploring Pennsylvania's Alleghenies

If you have read any of these vignettes and thought "I'd like to experience that myself!" then my goal has been accomplished—at least in that instance. Life in Pennsylvania's Allegheny Mountains can be richly sensorial, culturally fascinating and spiritually uplifting. But while you may be able to appreciate this region's qualities from your recliner, direct exposure to them will be so much more meaningful! That's why the the columns published in the newspaper usually mention events or sites that relate to the subject matter. Often, the columns offer telephone numbers, websites and other information to encourage you to sample the Alleghenies' natural and cultural heritage for yourself.

Carrying that component of the newspaper column over into this book format prompted much thought and discussion. Information changes so quickly in these dynamic days. Phone numbers go out of service. Websites go off-line. Events end, change their name, dates or sponsoring organizations. How could I provide you with information that encourages you to explore Pennsylvania's Alleghenies that wouldn't date the book and would give it a useful shelf life of several years?

Fortunately, we live in a day of increasingly sophisticated readers and Internet search engines. So the solution proved to be simple. What follows, in alphabetical order, is a listing of organizations, heritage venues and events that are referenced in the vignettes, along with a basic description that ensures you've found the reference for which you were looking. Simply plug the name into your favorite search engine, and you should find current

Appendix

information about that event, site or organization, whether you do so today or several years from now. So let the Internet be your guide to the natural and cultural resources of Pennsylvania's Allegheny Mountains. There has never been a better time to enjoy America's first frontier!

A

(The) Alleghenies Tourism Confederation (541 58th Street, Altoona, PA, 16602): an organization promoting ATV riding, bicycling, birding, boating, diving, fishing, hiking and motor touring in Bedford, Blair, Cambria, Centre, Fulton, Huntingdon and Somerset Counties.

Allegheny Mountains Convention and Visitors Bureau (1 Convention Center Drive, Altoona, PA, 16602): a resource for attractions, sites and events in Blair County.

Allegheny Portage Railroad National Historic Site (110 Federal Park Road, Gallitzin, PA, 16641): interprets Pennsylvania Main Line Canal themes.

Armstrong County Tourism Bureau (125 Market Street, Kittanning, PA, 16201): a resource for attractions, sites and events.

B

Bedford County Visitors Bureau (131 South Juliana Street, Bedford, PA, 15522): a resource for attractions, sites and events.

Blairsville Underground Railroad Museum (214 East Lane, Blairsville, PA, 15717).

Bottle Works Ethnic Arts Center (411 Third Avenue, Johnstown, PA, 15906).

Broad Top Area Coal Miners Historical Society and Museum (South Main Street, Robertsdale, PA, 16674).

Bushy Run Battlefield (Route 993, Jeanette, PA, 15644): hosts an annual reenactment of the 1763 battle over the first weekend of August each year.

C

Cambria County Historical Society (615 North Center Street, Ebensburg, PA, 15931): a repository for records of Welsh settlement in America and Cambria County.

Central Pennsylvania Convention and Visitors Bureau (800 East Park Avenue, State College, PA, 16803): a resource for attractions, sites and events in Centre County.

Exploring Pennsylvania's Alleghenies

Coal and Coke Heritage Center, Penn State Fayette Campus (1 University Drive, Uniontown, PA, 15401).

Compass Inn (1382 Route 30, Laughlintown, PA, 15655): a museum located in a circa 1799 stagecoach stop.

Conemaugh River Lake (1665 Auen Road, Saltsburg, PA, 15681): a flood-protection dam and recreation area operated by the U.S. Army Corps of Engineers, featuring Main Line Canal traces at the Tunnelview Historic Site.

D

David Bradford House (175 South Main Street, Washington, PA, 15301): an eighteenth- and early nineteenth-century historical site that interprets a Whiskey Rebellion story.

F

Fort Ligonier (200 South Market Street, Ligonier, PA, 15658): recreated fort and museum with an extensive collection of eighteenth-century paintings, artifacts and period-correct artillery; also the site of Fort Ligonier Days, commemorating the battle of October 12, 1758, annually on the second weekend in October.

Fort Necessity National Battlefield (1 Washington Parkway, Farmington, PA, 15437): has a visitor's center in partnership with the National Road Heritage Corridor and hosts commemorative activities over the Fourth of July weekend each year.

Fort Pitt Museum (101 Commonwealth Place, Point State Park, Pittsburgh, PA, 15222): interprets the struggle between the British and French for control of this gateway to the west.

Friendship Hill National Historic Site (223 New Geneva Road, Point Marion, PA, 15474): interprets the home and life of Albert Gallatin.

Fulton County Tourism Council (201 Lincoln Way West, McConnellsburg, PA, 17233): a resource for attractions, sites and events.

G

Great Allegheny Passage: a walking, bicycling and equestrian (on limited sections) trail extending from Pittsburgh to Cumberland, MD. At Cumberland, the trail connects with the C&O Canal Towpath that continues to Washington, D.C.

Appendix

Greater Johnstown/Cambria County Convention and Visitor's Bureau (416 Main Street, Suite 100, Johnstown, PA, 15901): a resource for attractions, sites and events.

Greater Pittsburgh Convention and Visitors Bureau, Regional Enterprise Tower (425 Sixth Avenue, Thirtieth Floor, Pittsburgh, PA, 15219): a resource for attractions, sites and events in Allegheny County.

H

Hanna's Town (809 Forbes Trail Road, Greensburg, PA, 15601): a recreated frontier village that was Westmoreland County's first county seat.

Heinz Regional History Center (1212 Smallman Street, Pittsburgh, PA, 15222): its permanent or long-term exhibits cover the French and Indian War, glassmaking in the region, regional innovations, western Pennsylvania sports, the H.J. Heinz Company and ethnic group collections.

Horseshoe Curve National Historic Landmark (Glenwhite Road, Altoona, PA, 16601).

Huntingdon County Visitors Bureau (6993 Seven Points Road, Suite 2, Hesston, PA, 16647): a resource for attractions, events and sites including Raystown Lake.

I

Idlewild Park (Route 30 East, Ligonier, PA, 15638).

Indiana County Tourist Bureau (2334 Oakland Avenue, Indiana, PA, 15701): a resource for attractions, sites and events.

J

Johnstown Flood Museum (304 Washington Street, Johnstown, PA, 15901).

Johnstown Flood National Memorial (733 Lake Road, South Fork, PA, 15956): interprets the flood and the South Fork Fishing and Hunting Club historic district.

Johnstown Heritage Discovery Center (201 Sixth Avenue, Johnstown, PA, 15906): interprets steelmaking, immigration and ethnicity themes and includes a children's museum.

K

Kennywood Park (4800 Kennywood Boulevard, West Mifflin, PA, 15122).

Exploring Pennsylvania's Alleghenies

L

Lakemont Park (700 Park Avenue, Altoona, PA, 16602).

Laurel Highlands (120 East Main Street, Ligonier, PA, 15658): a resource for attractions, sites and events in Fayette, Somerset and Westmoreland Counties.

LeMoyne House (49 East Maiden Street, Washington, PA, 15301): an Underground Railroad site that also interprets early nineteenth-century life.

Lower Trail: a multiuse rail-trail that extends for sixteen miles along the Frankstown Branch of the Juniata River from Flowing Spring in Blair County to Alexandria in Huntingdon County.

M

Mount Union Church (Turkeyfoot Trail, Rockwood, PA, 15557): home of the Sacred Harp Singers.

Mount Washington Observatory (2779 White Mountain Highway, North Conway, NH, 03860): a valuable resource for weather lore and information.

N

National Road Heritage Corridor (1 Washington Parkway, Farmington, PA, 15437): has a visitor's center in partnership with Fort Necessity National Battlefield.

O

Old Bedford Village (220 Sawblade Road, Bedford, PA, 15522): features authentic buildings of the late eighteenth and early nineteenth centuries and schedules reenactment events for a variety of historical periods throughout the summer.

Old St. Luke's Church (330 Washington Pike, Carnegie, PA, 15106): a historical site that traces its roots to 1765 and interprets colonial and Whiskey Rebellion themes.

Oliver Miller Homestead (Buffalo Drive, South Park, PA, 15129): a historical site that interprets eighteenth-century frontier life and the Whiskey Rebellion.

Appendix

P

Pennsylvania Bituminous Coal Show: an annual event in Carmichaels, Green County, sponsored by the King Coal Association.

Pennsylvania Department of Conservation and Natural Resources: administers state parks and forests.

Pennsylvania Maple Festival (120 Meyers Ave., Meyersdale, PA, 15552).

Pennsylvania State Forests: includes Buchanan, Forbes, Gallitzin, Rothrock and Tuscarora.

Pennsylvania State Parks: includes Blue Knob, Canoe Creek, Cowans Gap, Greenwood Furnace, Keystone, Kooser, Laurel Hill, Laurel Mountain, Laurel Ridge, Laurel Summit, Linn Run, Ohiopyle, Prince Gallitzin, Shawnee, Trough Creek, Warriors Path, Whipple Dam and Yellow Creek.

Pioneer Historical Society of Bedford County (242 East John Street, Bedford, PA, 15522).

Q

Quecreek Mine Rescue Site (151 Haupt Road, Somerset, PA, 15501).

R

Railroaders Memorial Museum (1300 Ninth Avenue, Altoona, PA, 16602): interprets life in a Pennsylvania Railroad town and operates the Horseshoe Curve National Historic Landmark.

River sojourns scheduled annually: Alle-Kiski-Connie Sojourn, Juniata River Sojourn and Stonycreek-Kiski-Conemaugh Sojourn.

S

Saint David's Society of Pittsburgh: preserves and presents Welsh heritage and maintains the Welsh Nationality Room at the Cathedral of Learning, University of Pittsburgh (4200 Fifth Avenue, Pittsburgh, PA, 15260).

Saints Peter and Paul Ukrainian Orthodox Church (200 Walnut Street, Carnegie, PA, 15106): has an annual pysanky sale.

Seldom Seen Tourist Mine (353 Seldom Seen Road, Hastings, PA, 16646).

Shaver's Creek Environmental Center (3400 Discovery Road, Petersburg, PA, 16669).

Somerset Historical Center (10649 Somerset Pike, Somerset, PA, 15501): interprets the rural life of the Allegheny Plateau and hosts an annual pioneer crafts festival called Mountain Craft Days.

Exploring Pennsylvania's Alleghenies

U

United States National Park Service: administers Allegheny Portage Railroad National Historic Site, Fort Necessity National Battlefield, Friendship Hill National Historic Site and Johnstown Flood National Memorial.

W

The War that Made America: a four-hour dramatic documentary that explains how the French and Indian War laid the groundwork for the American Revolution.

Washington County Tourism Promotion Agency (273 South Main Street, Washington, PA, 15301): a resource for attractions, sites and events.

Westmoreland Heritage, University of Pittsburgh at Greensburg (1150 Mount Pleasant Road, Greensburg, PA, 15601): works with other groups to preserve and present Westmoreland County history and co-sponsors the annual Arthur St. Clair Lecture.

West Penn Trail: a multiuse trail extending nineteen miles from Blairsville to Saltsburg that features traces of the Main Line Canal and Pennsylvania Railroad.

Westsylvania Petition: the effort by two thousand frontiersmen to create a new state in 1776.

Windber Coal Heritage Center (501 Fifteenth Street, Windber, PA, 15963): cosponsors an annual Miners' Memorial Day weekend.

Woodville Plantation (1375 Washington Pike, Bridgeville, PA, 15017): interprets the 1780–1820 period and the Whiskey Rebellion.

About the Author

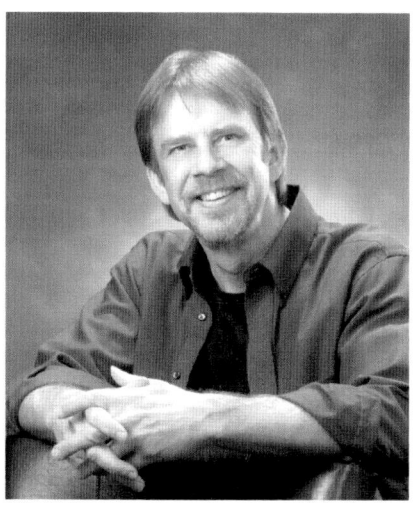

In deference to true writers, Dave Hurst considers himself a "wordwright"—simply a craftsman who works with words. As such, he has been researching and writing about the regional heritage of south-central and southwestern Pennsylvania for twenty-five years— first as a journalist, then as the founder and editor of *Westsylvania* magazine and now as a freelancer. In his weekly newspaper column, Dave combines his interests in the region's history, natural attributes and cultural heritage with his love of outdoor activities in ways intended to inspire readers to experience and celebrate Pennsylvania's Allegheny Mountains. His columns can be read at www.hurstmediaworks.com.

Visit us at
www.historypress.net

This title is also available as an e-book